Corporate Social Responsibility and Leadership

Legal, Ethical, and Practical Considerations for the Global Business Leader

Frank J. Cavico

ILEAD Academy, LLC
Davie, Florida. United States of America
www.ileadacademy.com

Frank J. Cavico, 2014. *Corporate Social Responsibility and Leadership: Legal, Ethical, and Practical Considerations for the Global Business Leader*

Technical Production Manager: Bahaudin G. Mujtaba
Cover Design by: Cagri Tanyar

© ILEAD Academy, LLC

ISBN-13: 978-1-936237-09-8

ISBN-10: 1-936237-09-1

Subject Code & Description
    BUS008000 - Business & Economics: Business Ethics
    LAW036000 - Law: Ethics and Professional Responsibility
    BUS094000 - Business & Economics: Green Business
    PHI005000 - Philosophy: Ethics & Moral Philosophy

Printed in the United States of America by ILEAD Academy, LLC. Davie, Florida.

★ International ★
ILEAD ACADEMY
Leadership Education and Associate Development Academy

Dedication

This book is dedicated to those law-abiding,
ethical and socially responsible
professionals around the globe!

Table of Contents

Preface

We believe that business leaders – whether entrepreneur, CEO, executive, officer, or manager- must act in a legal, ethical, and socially responsible manner. As such, business leaders in pursuing profits must obey the law, act for the greater good, treat all stakeholders with dignity and respect, and in a prudent manner be socially responsible by contributing to charities and participating in and supporting community and civic activities. Acting in such a responsible way will require business leaders to be cognizant of various stakeholder interests as well as to seek to balance these at times conflicting constituencies in a fair and efficacious manner. This objective is a challenging one, indeed, but also a noble one. Yet the result will be the creation of long-term, sustainable value, not "merely" for the shareholders but also for the employees, customers, communities, and all the stakeholders of the organization, including society as a whole.

The recent real estate/mortgage/banking crisis in the United States, resulting in the still recessionary U.S. economy, was in main part created by so-called business "leaders" abandoning common sense, good sense, and ethics, and consequently acting in a short-term, solely profit-centered, immoral, if not downright illegal, manner. Instead of earning rewards fairly, the prevailing mentality was a get-rich-quick one, exacerbated by the false belief that the price of real estate would go up – forever! Consequently, people with "NINJA" loans, that is, with no income, no jobs, or assets borrowed money that they realistically could never repay to buy over-appraised houses; and then so-called (yet too accurately called) "sub-prime" mortgages were "securitized" into basically fraudulent securities, though securities rated as "safe" ones, which were sold to unsuspecting buyers. The result was a financial disaster and economic "meltdown," which the nation and many people are still suffering from. Throughout the political, economic, business, banking, real estate, and mortgage fields, short-sighted, if not immoral, business people tolerated undue risks, illegal, "borderline" legal, and clearly unethical conduct. Individualistic, risky, short-term, profit-seeking – from real estate agents, mortgage brokers, and bankers - was the "moral" norm; and the deleterious effect on society of this misbehavior did not even register. The result was a massive destruction of value – short- and long-term – the ruination of businesses, business and personal assets, and people's lives, necessitating massive taxpayer "bailouts," and engendering a serious undermining of confidence in the U.S. economic and political system.

Capitalism and free markets are built on, as Adam Smith wisely stated long ago, a foundation of morality. The economy needs to be free to function, but the economy also needs rules to function correctly and effectively. And when the legal rules are not present or they are not clear, there is all the more need for ethics and socially responsible behavior. The idea is to create a sustainable form of capitalism, whereby acting in a legal, ethical, and socially responsible manner, as well as taking a long-term perspective, will produce profits for the shareholders but also long-term value for all the other stakeholders of the company. The task of business leaders, therefore, is to incorporate not only legal rules but also ethical, social responsibility, and stakeholder considerations into corporate values, mission statements, governance policy, and strategy, and to do so not "just" nationally but globally. Transparency, truthfulness, and trustworthiness have been, are, should be, and must be the hallmarks of successful American business; business managers have a moral obligation to be trustees of all the stakeholders of the organization; yet, sadly, these moral lessons now must be learned once again. A true business leader must be keenly aware and engaged, must look ahead, and must foresee the consequences of his or her company's actions on all the firm's stakeholders, including society as a whole. Business leaders must be aware that law, ethics, and social responsibility are all interconnected and underpin the economy and the free market system.

The book supplies a reminder, a rationale, and a guide for legal, ethical, and socially responsible behavior, as well as a warning of the "fruits from the poisonous tree"; and consequently the author also hopes that the book serves as a tool for true business success, stakeholder responsibility, and organizational and societal sustainability. Capitalism, yes; but a capitalism "regulated" and tempered by law, ethics, morality, and social responsibility; and thus a capitalism with a "communitarian spirit" or, in the words of the Venetians long-ago (yet still quite true), a "communally controlled capitalism"; and as per the Venetian motto and cardinal maxim - "All for the honor *and* profit of Venice" (emphasis added!).

Frank

CHAPTER 1

Introduction

Business is all about values. One core value is obviously the economic one, that is, business is expected to be profitable and to make money for the owners, shareholders, and investors. However, business is further expected to achieve this economic value in conformity with the value of legality, but also, since the law may be non-existent, deficient, vague, or not enforced, with the value of morality. That is, business must act in a profitable, legal, and moral manner.

Book Overview
Today, moreover, business must deal with another value – the expectation that business, as it grows and especially once it attains a certain size, wealth, and prominence, be "socially responsible." As such, above and beyond the responsibility to act legally and morally in the pursuit of profit is the notion of social responsibility, which typically today in a business context is called "corporate social responsibility" (CSR). The law defines legal accountability; ethics determines moral accountability; but ascertaining the definition, nature, extent of, and rationale for the value social responsibility emerges as an even more challenging task.

This work, therefore, takes a legal, philosophical, as well as practical approach, to explaining and illustrating the concept of social responsibility in a modern-day, global, business environment. The notion of the social responsibility of business has several components – legal, ethical, spiritual, philanthropic, sustainability, reputational, and practical, all of which will be explicated by the author and the contributors to this book. The legal aspect of social responsibility will be addressed "above and beyond" the basic legal level of compliance with the law by means of an examination of corporate "constituency" statutes in the United States as well as an examination of a new corporate legal formulation, in the U.S. as well as other countries, of the "social benefit" corporation. Social responsibility can also form part of the subject of "corporate governance," and accordingly the author and contributors will examine the social responsibility ramifications of corporate governance.

There are 18 chapters to this book. After this *Introduction* in *Chapter 1*, the author in *Chapter 2, The Values of Legality, Morality, and Social Responsibility*, defines certain key terms, which the author in the spirit of Socrates refers to as "definitional principles," to wit: values, intrinsic values, instrumental values, law, legality, philosophy, ethics, morality, and social responsibility. Intrinsic values are differentiated from instrumental values; and legality, morality, and social responsibility are also differentiated. The author emphasizes that it is critical to know these concepts and to keep these terms and concepts separate and distinct for analytical purposes. In *Chapter 3, The Ethical Principle of Last Resort*, the author further distinguishes morality from social responsibility by explaining and illustrating an ethical principle related to, but distinct from, social responsibility, that deals with the moral duty to act, to help, to aid, and to rescue – the Ethical Principle of Last Resort. The author then explains how this traditional ethical principle differs from the more modern concept of "social responsibility." *Chapter 4, The Sophists*, takes a more philosophical approach to social responsibility by going back to Ancient Greece and the philosophical school of the Sophists and further explicating intrinsic values from instrumental values, and demonstrating, in the context of social responsibility, the worth of such a value, even if it is designated as a "mere" instrumental one. The author underscores the practical aspects of social responsibility; and accordingly provide rationales why the discerning business leader should take a "sophisticated" approach to social responsibility in the business realm. In *Chapter 5, Social Responsibility: Corporate Social Responsibility in the United States*, the authors first trace the history of the concept of "social responsibility" as applied to business; next the authors provide definitions of the term – ranging from the "merely" philanthropic to "stakeholder" to "sustainability"; and then the authors provide several illustrations of corporate social responsibility in the United States, underscoring the "strategic" approaches that business leaders use in devising and implementing social responsibility initiatives for business. The authors also stress the practical benefits of a firm being regarded as a "socially responsible" one. *Chapter 6, Corporate Social Responsibility: Global Perspectives*, takes a similar approach to the preceding chapter but naturally focuses on corporate social responsibility in an international context. Again, the instrumental, strategic, and beneficial value of corporate social responsibility is emphasized. *Chapter 7, Socially Responsible Investing*, provides a discussion of a new form of investment vehicle – social responsibility funds - for the socially responsible investor. In this chapter, the authors also provide information as to socially responsible rating organizations and websites for the discerning, socially responsible investor. Commencing in *Chapter 8, Corporate "Constituency" Statutes*, the author takes a more legalistic approach to the subject of social responsibility by examining state corporation statutes in the United States, typically called "constituency" statutes, which allow corporate boards of directors to consider in corporate policy- and decision-making the interests of other constituent groups, that is, stakeholders, who are affected by the corporation, including local communities and society as a whole. The author points out that these constituency statutes were the legal means by which corporate directors were allowed to, and thus could, engage in social responsibility efforts for stakeholders above and beyond satisfying the interests of the shareholders. In *Chapter 9, Social Benefit Corporations*, the authors discuss a new form of doing business as a corporation in the United States – the social benefit corporation or "B-corp," whereby the directors of the company must consider the interests and values of stakeholders in addition to the shareholders, including society as a whole. Accordingly, the authors discuss the corporate laws of certain states in the U.S. which now allow a business to incorporate or change its charter to achieve "social benefit" status. In particular, in addition to the obvious social benefits of a corporation being a "B-corp," the authors also point out certain legal risks for directors who serve on the board of a social benefit corporation. Related to the social benefit corporation is the Low-Profit Limited Liability Company, or L3C, which is a very recent development in social business formation. So, in *Chapter 10, Low-Profit Limited Liability Companies (L3Cs)*, the author discusses this new organization, which has just been adopted by a few states in the U.S.; and the author also points out the risky tax ramifications today of doing business as an L3C. In *Chapter 11, Social Responsibility and Corporate Governance*, the author discusses the modern concept of corporate governance. The author takes an expansive approach to defining and explicating "corporate governance" by addressing not only the legal but also the ethical and social responsibility ramifications of corporate governance for the business leader today.

Chapter 12, CSR, and the Advantages of Going Green, contributed by a colleague of the authors, examines the relationship of corporate social responsibility to taking "green" initiatives along with its overall benefits to the company and society. *Chapter 13, CSR and Human Resource Management in a Spiritual Context*, also contributed by a colleague of the authors, provides a religious component to the discussion of corporate social responsibility as well as an Islamic model of human resource management.

Based on the all the foregoing discussion, examples, and analysis, in *Chapter 14, Implications and Recommendations for "Socially Responsible" Business Leaders*, the author discusses the ramifications for a business being regarded as a socially responsible versus a socially non-responsive or socially irresponsible business. The author emphasizes the importance today of a business in fact being regarded as a socially responsible as well as a legal and moral entity; and the authors demonstrate how a business can be socially responsible in a smart, strategic, prudent, and instrumental manner; and thereby the business can benefit not only the shareholders but also other stakeholders, including society as a whole. In order to help the business leader make shrewd, socially responsible business decisions, in *Chapter 15, Stakeholder Values*, the author discusses the stakeholders or constituent groups affected by the business, what these stakeholders value, and how the business leader must balance these values in making socially responsible decisions in an advantageous manner for the business and all the stakeholders. This chapter also presents a *"Table of Stakeholder Values"* to illustrate the considerations involved in socially responsible decision-making. In *Chapter 16, The Business Sustainability Continuum*, the authors present a model of sustainability for business, which they call the *"Business Sustainability Continuum"* (BSC). The BSC illustrates and explains four key values for business – the practical, legal, ethical, and socially responsible – and shows how they are distinct, yet related in the sense that they flow into as well as reinforce one into another, in order to achieve a level of continual success for business – and success that is not only beneficial for the business but for all its stakeholders, including society as a whole.

The next topic to the book is *Chapter 17, Motivation for Social and Environmental Responsibility*, contributed by a colleague of the authors, which focused on why some leaders choose to champion social and environmentally positive initiatives. Some leaders become environmentally conscious because of a "whack on the head", others might have a "squeeze of the heart" and some may feel the urgency to put their "hands in action" or things will not improve. The last chapter to the book is *Chapter 18, Conclusion*, whereby the author provides a brief summary; and then concludes by extolling the benefits to the company and all its stakeholders as well as society of the firm being a socially responsible business; but "socially responsible" construed in a "sophisticated" sense, that is, in a smart, strategic, shrewd, prudent, and instrumental manner. The objective, the author emphasizes, is to do well by doing good! Finally, an extensive *Bibliography* is provided followed by brief *Biographies* of the author and contributors.

Summary
This chapter provided a brief introduction to corporate social responsibility and initially explained why business leaders around the globe should act in a socially responsible manner. Global business leaders are likely to face many decisions that will impact themselves, their companies, employees, and colleagues, as well as their family members, local communities, and society in general. As such, it is

incumbent upon academics, business and corporate leaders, community leaders, and government regulators to help business people to understand corporate social responsibility so that they can act accordingly in best interest of the business entity and all its relevant stakeholders.

CHAPTER 2

The Values of Legality, Morality, and Social Responsibility

The author and contributors of this book firmly believe that one must be as precise as possible when engaging in analysis, particularly ethical analysis. Accordingly, the author believes that it is very harmful for people to use continually a wide variety of very general terms, especially terms intending to describe moral ideas. Even more dangerous is an extreme personal relativism, that is, the notion that such terms as "justice" have no basis in reality and consequently that whatever any person thought was just was "just" for him or her. The lack of any fixed meaning, the inability of people to provide proper explanations, individualistic and expedient decision-making, and an emphasis on rhetoric and persuasion engender relativism, skepticism, and a great deal of confusion, particularly in the meanings attached to moral terms. Perhaps the Relativists are right and the terms have no meaning; but if so, then people should not use them. Yet, if the terms do have permanent, objective meaning, then the people who do use them ought to be able to say what they mean. It is not only wrong, but also quite unhelpful, to discuss whether a person's conduct was just or unjust, moral or immoral, or good or bad unless there is some agreement as to what justice, morality, and goodness are. If there is no agreement, people may use the same words to mean different things. They then will be talking at cross-purposes and their discussions will make no progress, either intellectually or morally. Only confusion, skepticism, chaos, and perhaps even conflict, will ensue.

Therefore, it is very important for a business leader, academic, and manager to look for, ascertain, and pay special attention to definitions and terms. When one initially encounters the field of social responsibility in a business context, one is confronted with some confusion due to a lack of an agreed-upon terminology and set of definitions. What is social responsibility? How does it differ from the law, ethics, and morality? What exactly do the terms "corporate social responsibility," "stakeholder values," "sustainability," "people, planet, and profits," "going green," and "socially responsible investing" mean? What is a corporate "constituency" statute and how does it compare and contrast to a "social benefit corporation"? As such, if one is going to understand what social responsibility is, and how it works in a modern global business environment, there must be some agreement on, and some insight into, the meaning and nature of the value of social responsibility, especially when juxtaposed with the values of legality, based on the law, and the value of morality, based on ethics. There is, therefore, a need for words, terms, and definitions with precise meaning. Definitions also can function as "definitional principles," that is, the "first principles" of reasoning to conclusions. If one defines terms carefully at the start, or knows the appropriate definitions, and one applies them consistently, one can draw moral conclusions deductively from these fundamental "first principles." One, therefore, can use definitions and terms to decide what to do in particular cases. In order to arrive at a precise as possible meaning of the term "social responsibility," it is first necessary to define related fundamental terms and concepts.

"Values" are rankings or priorities that a person establishes for one's norms and beliefs. Values express what the chief end of life is, the highest good, and what things in life are worthwhile or desirable. Deeply held values can drive behavior. One very difficult problem is placing values in proper relation to one another. An important distinction must be made between two types of values: instrumental and intrinsic values. "Instrumental" (also called "extrinsic") values are good because of their consequences. They are desired as a means to an end. Their worth is not in their own right, but because of what they can bring in the way of other values, for example, economic values. One illustration would be money, which is not good in and of itself, but rather as a tool or instrument to obtain other values, such as happiness. "Intrinsic" (also called "terminal") values, however, are good in and of themselves. They are an end in themselves and desired for their own sake. They are values that claim appraisal in their own right. They are, or claim to be, of absolute worth. Moral values are generally held to be intrinsic. Accordingly, if one holds morality to be an intrinsic value, then one must be moral regardless of the circumstances and consequences. Happiness is also posited as an intrinsic value. So, it seems that money can, and should, buy happiness.

A significant value for the business community today is the value of legality, which is obviously based on the law. Actually, when making or contemplating a business decision, one of the first determinations to be made is whether the action is legal based on the law. The law is the set of public, universal commands that are capable of being complied with, generally accepted, and enforced by sanctions. Law describes the ways in which people are required to act in their relationships with others in an organized society. One purpose of the law is to keep people's ambitions, self-interest, and greed, especially in a capitalistic society, in check and in moderation. Positive law is the law of a people's own making; it is the law laid down by legislative bodies, courts, and other governmental organs. Law must be declared publicly. It must be published and made accessible in advance to all so that people can know that they are bound. Trained professionals, however, may be necessary to interpret and explain law. Law must treat equally those with similar characteristics who are similarly situated. There is an aura of insistency and inevitability to law. It must define what one must do and forbear from doing. The law is not composed of expectations, suggestions, and petitions to act in a certain way. The law requires one to act in a certain way. Most laws, however, particularly those affecting business, are negative; that is, they require business not to act in a certain way. Law must be accessible to the people who are to be bound by it. Laws are not legitimate if they neither can be found nor understood by people. Laws, moreover, are not legitimate if they do not clearly specify in advance what actions lie under the domain of those laws. Law cannot be so incomprehensible that no one can obey it. Law also cannot be inconsistent. Legal requirements, for example, that contradict each other cannot be termed "law" because people obviously cannot obey both. Law generally must be obeyed. It cannot be so contrary to dominant public opinion that virtually no one will either obey or enforce the law. Most members of a society must voluntarily obey the law. Law consists of commands enforced by sanctions, political, physical, and economic, which the officials of the state are able to, and disposed to, inflict on those who fail to comply. The essence of law is coercion. The law also relies on persuasion, but ultimately on force. The purpose of legal sanctions is to motivate compliance. People must be made to understand that they will be compelled to obey the law or suffer some loss. If law is not enforced, or enforced so rarely that people forget about it, the law degenerates into a mere trap for the unwary or unlucky. Social responsibility is *not* the law.

Philosophy is the study and analysis of such deeply problematical and fundamental question, such as the nature of reality, thought, conduct, and morality. Ethics *is* a branch of philosophy. Social responsibility is *not* a branch of philosophy. Moral philosophy is the philosophical study of morality; it is the application of philosophy to moral thinking, moral conduct, and moral problems. Moral philosophy encompasses various theories that prescribe what is good for people and what is bad, what constitutes right and wrong, and what one ought to do and ought not to do. Moral philosophy offers ethical theories that provide a theoretical framework for making, asserting, and defending a moral decision. There is not one determinate set of ethical theories. Moral philosophy embraces a range of ethical perspectives and spends a great deal of time in analyzing the differences among these ethical views. Each ethical theory, however, does underscore some ultimate principle or set of principles that one is obligated to follow to ensure moral behavior and the good life. It is the effort to systematize ethically moral judgments and to establish and defend ethically moral beliefs and standards. Moral philosophy develops ethical frameworks for evaluating the merits of asserted moral positions. Moral philosophy attempts to establish logical thought processes that will determine if an action is right or wrong and seeks to find criteria by which to distinguish good conduct from bad conduct. Social responsibility is *not* a part of moral philosophy.

"Ethics" is the theoretical study of morality. Ethical theories are moral philosophical undertakings that contain bodies of formal, systematic, and ethical principles that are committed to the view that an asserted ethical theory can determine how one should morally think and act. Moral judgments are deducible from a hierarchy of ethical principles. It is the moral philosopher's task to articulate such ethical principles and to insist upon their proper application. Ethics is the sustained and reasoned attempt to determine what is morally right or wrong. Ethics is used to test the moral correctness of beliefs, practices, and rules. Ethics necessarily involves an effort both to define what is meant by morality and to justify the way of acting and living that is being advocated. Ethics proceeds from a conviction that moral disagreements and conflicts are resolvable rationally. There is one "right" answer to any moral dispute, and this answer can be reached through ethical reasoning. The purpose of ethics is to develop, articulate, and justify principles and techniques that can be used in specific situations where a moral determination must be made about a particular action or practice. When a decision involves a moral component, the decision necessarily encompasses moral rules and ethical principles.

"Morals" are beliefs or views as to what is right or wrong or good or bad. Moral norms are standards of behavior by which people are judged and that require, prohibit, or allow specific types of behavior. Moral rules are action-guiding or prescriptive statements about how people ought to behave or ought not to behave. Ethics deals with matters that are of serious consequence to human beings. Ethics affects human welfare and fulfillment in significant ways. People will be positively or negatively affected by moral decisions. Ethics, therefore, is concerned with conduct that can benefit or harm human beings. Morals fundamentally convey norms to human life. Moral standards enable resolution of disputes by providing acceptable justification for actions. If one bases a decision on a moral rule, and if the moral rule is based on and derived from an agreed-upon ethical principle, the decision should be publicly acceptable. It is a reasoned ethical conclusion directed toward what one ought or ought not to do. Morality, therefore, properly and accurately should be understood as a development of the ethical. Social responsibility is *not* part of ethics, *not* an ethical theory, *not* an ethical principle, and *not* a means to determine morals, morality, or moral precepts.

CHAPTER 3

The Ethical Principle of Last Resort:
The Moral Duty to Act v. Social Responsibility

Although it is beyond the scope of this book to fully examine the fields of ethics and morality, it is necessary to briefly discuss and illustrate one key ethical principle – The Ethical Principle of Last Resort – due to its relationship to, and at times confusion with, the value of social responsibility. When does one have a positive moral obligation to act? Acting morally may involve more than merely avoiding negative harm; acting morally also may require one to perform an affirmative positive action, even though legally one may not be required to take the action. The ethical principle of "last resort" indicates when one has a moral duty to act, to aid or help another, or to rescue. Pursuant to Last Resort, one morally must act when there is a need, proximity, capability, one is the last resort or chance to avoid the peril, and when acting would not cause harm, or threaten to cause harm, equal to or greater than the original peril. The principle is based partially on ethical admonition that "ought implies can," that is, that one is obligated to do only what one can do. Thus, if one is unable to act and help, due to lack of opportunity, means, or resources, one is not obligated morally to act.

The "Last Resort" principle usually involves an obligation of immediacy and high priority posed by an emergency; it thus generates a moral obligation to act that one cannot ignore without moral condemnation. The classic example is a drowning case when the five "last resort" factors are present. The problem in successfully applying the "last resort" principle to business, however, emerges the fourth and fifth factors. Who is the last resort for people unemployed and in need, business or government? Would business "rescuing" in fact harm the corporation, or its shareholders, or other stakeholders? A "friendly takeover," a corporation helping an employee pay his or her children's college tuition, may be praiseworthy actions, but are they morally required under the "last resort" principle? Is a corporation immoral for choosing not to act in the preceding circumstances? One example is the case of the Malden Mills Company, whose very compassionate owner rebuilt the facility after a fire without terminating any employees; but due in part to the added financial strain of keeping those employees, he forced his company to file for Chapter 11 bankruptcy protection in order to reorganize its finances, thereby resulting in a considerably, and permanently, diminished workforce. Another example concerns the large, multinational pharmaceutical companies who are providing for free or at greatly reduced cost their patented anti-AIDS drugs to African nations. It is not their legal obligation to give away their products. Yet are they so doing because it is their moral responsibility as the "rescuer" of "last resort" or due to perhaps to other social pressures? Similarly, corporations may not be the "last resort" to take care of their employees' disabled children, yet companies such as Toyota and Raytheon do provide assistance, for example, by hosting dinners with speakers and holding "networking" events, as well as expanding insurance coverage for "special needs" children. If not moral duty, what motivates these meritorious actions? A most interesting and thought-provoking example concerns Wal-Mart's very meritorious response to the Hurricane Katrina disaster in New Orleans and the Gulf Coast. Was Wal-Mart's "trucking in" tons of relief supplies (literally!) "merely" a socially responsible action, or was Wal-Mart the "last resort" to bring rapid relief to this devastated region of the country; and if the latter, what does that say about the government— all levels of government—federal, state, and local – in the U.S. that they could not rapidly supply emergency aid? Similarly, the Coca-Cola Company has joined the AIDs fight in Africa by offering to use Coke trucks to deliver the AIDs prevention drugs and fliers as well as free condoms throughout Africa, even to the remotest village (Higgins, 2001). Coke certainly does not have any legal obligation to bring AIDs drugs to Africans; Coke is not the last resort to bring

AIDs drugs to Africans so they are not morally obligated to do; yet nonetheless Coke is bringing AIDs drugs to Africans, which means, *ipso facto*, that Coke is a very socially responsible company (and one getting and deserving some very good publicity).

So, then, what exactly is this value of "social responsibility" since it is neither a legal, philosophical, ethical, or moral value? Although business may not have a moral responsibility, based on the principle of "last resort," to improve the quality of life in the community and society, business may be obligated by a standard of social responsibility to work for social as well as economic betterment. A corporation, as well as a person, can have a non-moral duty, the failure to perform, which is not a moral wrong; yet one can be held accountable for failure to perform a social obligation. The words "accountability" and "responsibility," of course, imply some sort of an obligation on the part of business to deal with social problems. "Obligation" suggests that society may demand that business act in a certain socially responsible ways; otherwise, perhaps, society will compel business by law to fulfill its social obligations. Social responsibility in the sense of "corporate social responsibility" generally means that a company is actively engaged in the community by contributing to and participating in civic and charitable affairs. A company is thus a "good corporate citizen" by engaging in these philanthropic and civic-minded activities that benefit the community and society as a whole even though the company neither has a legal or a moral obligation to help. This basic definition of social responsibility will be further explicated and illustrated in the following sections of this work. Social responsibility, therefore, is a value, and a value distinct from legality and morality; and all are values that business leaders and managers must be able to deal with in an effective and efficacious manner. However, to answer the seminal questions as to whether social responsibility is an intrinsic value or "merely" an extrinsic value, as well as why, how, and how much should a company be socially responsible, one must first examine the teachings of the Sophists of Ancient Greece.

CHAPTER 4

The Sophists: Intrinsic v. Instrumental Values

Today, the word "sophist" is an insult; and consequently to call someone a "sophist" or to accuse them of engaging in "sophistry" is to malign a person. Yet the word "sophist" originally carried neither negative connotation nor disparaging reference. It merely meant teacher, professor, intellectual, disseminator of ideas, or practitioner of wisdom. The Sophists emerged with distinction in the latter decades of the fifth century B.C. in Greece, a period marked by substantial political and social transformation. Democracy was politically rising, but the affluence and authority of the old aristocratic families had not yet receded. The ascendance and expansion of democracy afforded many political opportunities, provided one possessed not only intelligence and ambition but also the knowledge and skills to prevail over one's adversaries. The Sophists traveled from city to city, offering schooling and supplying education to those who could afford to pay. They professed a wide variety of skills and knowledge; those essential to success in law and politics were most in demand. As the Sophists journeyed throughout Greece and the Mediterranean, they came to know of and report on the many peoples and cultures of the ancient world; they perceived diverse customs, practices, religions, governments, laws, beliefs, and values. The Sophists' own views were far from uniform, but one can sense a predilection toward relativism permeating their thinking. The Sophists did not establish any particular philosophical school or even hold one set of opinions; rather, they came into prominence as a profession of itinerant teachers. Some were, in fact, well versed in philosophy, others knew science, astronomy, mathematics, music, rhetoric, language, grammar, and memory training. In Fifth Century B.C. Greece there were no universities, law schools, colleges, adult education centers, and no public provision for education. There were no professional lawyers. The parties to a lawsuit appeared in person and made their own presentation and argumentation to a panel of judges composed of lay persons chosen by lot. There clearly was a need for professional instruction. The Sophists were the first professional teachers in Greece. The emphasis in their teaching was to impart practical knowledge and to inculcate practical skills, especially in the areas of law and politics. They taught material that would be useful to their fee-paying students. They concentrated on the knowledge and skills that were essential to advance one's position in society. Rhetoric, for example, was a leading subject for aspiring politicians and potential "lawyers." The methodologies of the Sophists also varied. Some conducted conventional classes; others gave lectures to large or small groups; others employed discussion groups or seminars; and some held question and answer sessions. They spoke on prepared themes from a written text, invited questions and commentary from the audience, and conducted rhetorical exercises (especially structured to show how the most unpromising position could be maintained). Many young ambitious adults with the means to pay attended their presentations and were educated in this new "school" of self-awareness, self-satisfaction, and self-realization. The study of rhetoric was particularly useful in a society where a great deal depended upon the ability to influence public opinion and to advocate a position in the law courts. Persuasive public speaking was, and still is, an essential component to success, advancement, and the attainment of power. Rhetoric, therefore, was one subject that practically all the Sophists taught. They stressed the important lesson of speaking and arguing with equal clarity and cogency on both sides of an issue. The Sophists instructed their students to see both sides to a question, to recognize the virtues and defects of each position, to approve and disapprove with commensurate vigor, and especially to bolster up the weaker side so that it would seem stronger. Although the Sophists emphasized the art of disputation, they did not restrict their teaching to mere form and style. In showing how to argue for or against any position, the Sophists also treated the substance of what was being disputed, but only to the extent that such substantive knowledge would be efficacious to the art of argumentation. The Sophists were convinced that people could be persuaded of anything. The emphasis on rhetoric flowed naturally from this cynical sounding and potentially subversive belief. Although the Sophists were cognizant of ethics and philosophy, their ultimate objective was neither to make the student "good" in the moral sense of the term, nor to assist the student in searching for and attaining the "truth" on any matter. Their aim was to help the student become a good speaker and a good debater and to master all the skills that would make the student successful and dominant in whatever sphere he or she endeavored to enter. The Sophists, viewed in this "sophisticated" light, conceivably can be pictured as the first business consultants, political promoters, and public relations specialists!

Protagoras (born 500 B.C.), an important figure in the Sophist fellowship, is credited with the saying: "Man is the measure of all things." This statement was interpreted to mean that everything is relative to each individual person; that everything is as it seems to each individual person; and that each person has the right to determine for himself or herself what is good and bad; and that what one considers good, another may consider bad. Consequently, there is no intrinsic truth or value – to anything! Obviously, such an interpretation leads one down a relativistic path. Morality since it possesses no intrinsic value is "merely" relative to the particular perceiver or actor. There are no absolute and intrinsic values, general principles, fundamental rules, or objective standards as to what is right and wrong, good or bad, and proper or improper. When people differ on issues, there are no impersonal criteria to decide who is right and who is wrong. Truth, moral or otherwise, is individual and temporary, not intrinsic, universal, and eternal. Truth for any person is simply what he or she believes for the moment or what he or she could be convinced of; and the Sophists maintained that it was possible to persuade anyone of anything.

Nevertheless, despite the fact that the Sophists were total relativists who denied the intrinsic value of religion, legality, justice, morality, and ethics, recall that values can be either intrinsic or "merely" instrumental or extrinsic. The Sophists, of course, adjured any intrinsic value. Yet they did place value – very practical value – on the instrumental nature of values. That is, certain values, though not intrinsically true, may be quite relative to advancing a person's self-interest and thus be viewed as instruments or tools to serve and promote one's egoistic endeavors. These values then possessed instrumental value to the Sophists. To illustrate, take religion, which to the Sophists had no intrinsic value or truth, but which could be used instrumentally to advance one's self-interest. As such, the Sophists would teach "courses" in religion, though they did not believe intrinsically in God or religion or any religion. They would teach courses in religion (Greek, Roman, Persian, Egyptian – whatever) because they believed that religion might be a useful tool for a person to promote and advance himself or herself, for example, by appearing righteous, making good (especially business) contacts through religion, ingratiating oneself in a religious community, or not losing a deal or business opportunity by inadvertently insulting someone's religion. Religion, therefore, even if lacking in intrinsic value or truth, nonetheless should not be jettisoned as it might be relative to a person and could be used, along with the rhetorical skills and the other subjects the Sophists taught, as beneficial, egoistic instruments. To further illustrate, take morality and ethics: the Sophists taught both subject matters; yet as with religion they did not believe there was any intrinsic truth or value to, or objective and universal standard of, morality and ethics; they were merely relative terms and concepts. Yet morality and ethics might possess some value and worth – instrumental value and worth – said the Sophists. That is, morality and ethics might be relative to a person's quest for power, position, or money. For example, if one wants to be a leader, say a business leader, one will need followers; and these followers will have to be convinced that the leader's vision is an inherently moral one; so knowing some ethics will be quite helpful indeed instrumentally to convince people that one is a moral leader worthy of following. Similarly, if one, for example, an aspirant for political or corporative executive position or power, or perhaps an aspiring entrepreneur, is accused of acting immorally, what will one do? Nothing, and risk censure? Or will one defend one's action as moral? The latter, of course, but in order to defend oneself against an accusation of immorality, one needs to be well-versed in ethics. And the Sophists of Ancient Greece would be more than happy (for a fee, of course) to teach one some ethics. As with religion, one should not toss out morality and ethics but rather use them as tools of instrumental value and worth to help one achieve one's goals.

One now can discern the more modern definition of the term "sophist" emerging, with its negative connotations of overly clever but false argumentation and disingenuous reasoning. As one can perceive, the Sophists shocked people, especially people for whom philosophy, ethics, morality, and law were a way of life closely tied to religion. To many people, the Sophists seemed to be overly clever and cynical contrivers who made use of specious and disingenuous disputations. To some people, they appeared as utterly immoral; and these perceptions, perhaps, were the origins of the odium that the Sophists incurred and the reasons for the negative connotations of the term "sophistry." The Sophists, however, did demonstrate intellectual merit. They vigorously pursued their studies, setting aside what was traditionally thought as morally, culturally, and legally "right" and edifying.

An example of the Sophist's advice that "virtue comes from having money" could be the case of John D. Rockefeller, who had a very bad reputation during the Gilded Age as a monopolist and "robber baron," until a public relations person told him that civic and charitable donations could help salvage his damaged image. Similarly, Andrew Carnegie was known as one of the greatest philanthropists in the U.S., because he was involved early on in his career in very socially responsible activities, especially funding libraries. The interesting, and paradoxical, point about Carnegie is that he apparently enjoyed giving away his money, and being regarded as a benefactor to society, so much that he engaged in even more ruthless, monopolistic, illegal, and unethical business actions, such as industrial violence, bribery, price-fixing, and tax fraud, so as to make more money so he would have more wealth to distribute and thus burnish his reputation as a benefactor to society. He thus did "bad" to do "good." So, the question emerges: Did the Carnegie "means" justify the "ends"?

CHAPTER 5

Social Responsibility: CSR in the USA[1]

What exactly is a corporation's "social responsibility"? Does a corporation have a social obligation to take care of the poor, educate the public, give to charity, and fund cultural programs? Social projects and social welfare in the United States traditionally have been viewed as the appropriate domain of government, not of business. Business, of course, is taxed and such taxes may be used for social purposes. The traditional purpose of business as viewed in the U.S., moreover, is the profitable production and distribution of goods and services, not social welfare. Yet by raising the issue of social responsibility, business is forced to concern itself with the "social" dimension of its activities.

The conservative Republican and University of Chicago professor, as well as Nobel Laureate, Milton Friedman, took a very narrow and "legalistic" of view of social responsibility in a business context. Friedman believed that the social responsibility of business is to make money – legally – and pay taxes. The role of the corporation is to create jobs, goods, services, and wealth; and any civic or charitable endeavors beyond that function are the choice of the individuals working for and owning the corporation – the employees and shareholders. It is not the role of the corporation to solve the world's social problems. Corporate profits should go to the shareholders – the owners of the company and not be spent on social causes. Individual charitable efforts are best effectuated by wealth, and wealth is best created by a free market unencumbered by

---

[1] Coauthored with Bahaudin G. Mujtaba, Nova Southeastern University.

government regulation, moral persuasion, and social responsibility expectations. Declared Milton Friedman, the social responsibility of business is to increase profits! A recent, and perhaps surprising, advocate of a Milton Friedman conservative view of social responsibility is the former Clinton Administration Labor Secretary, and liberal Democrat, Robert B. Reich. Reich believes that his fellow "liberals" are wrong to continually urge companies to be socially responsible. Corporations are not set up to be social institutions, Reich declared, in agreement with Friedman. Corporate CEOs have not been conferred with the authority or the legitimacy to determine where the public interest lies and to set and fulfill social objectives, Reich says. Rather, elected and representative government officials should make these value determinations for society, and then promulgate specific laws and rules for private sector companies to follow and then to use and direct them to help fulfill social goals. Furthermore, in a very controversial declaration, Reich contends that in essence it really does not make sense to criticize, and even to praise, companies for being socially responsible, environmentally conscious, or a "good employer." Why? Do not believe for a moment, Reich states, that a company will sacrifice profits for the sake of social goals. Yet, it could be argued that Reich's profit rationale is a short-sighted one, since it very well could be argued that not only are profits not antithetical to social responsibility, but a firm's long-term commitment to social responsibility can materially enhance profits.

The concept of the social responsibility for business was first introduced by the prominent scholar, Adolf Berle, in his 1932 text, co-authored with Gardner Means, *The Modern Corporation and Private Property*, wherein the notions of community and stakeholder interest, service to the public, "trusteeship" to non-shareholder constituencies, stabilization of business, as well as a broader social understanding of corporations, were raised. However, Berle did not elaborate how the corporation should determine what this community interest is or how it should be advanced; but nonetheless scholars claim Berle "helped start" the debate over corporate social responsibility. Similarly, Mickels (2009, p. 273) states that "this debate raised the question of whether corporations owed a duty of 'trusteeship" to constituencies other than shareholders." And this debate over the social responsibility of business, they emphasize, "…is not a relic of the past; it is alive and well" (Page and Katz, 2011, p.1360).

Accordingly, what is the "social responsibility" of business today? The term at a basic philanthropic level may be defined as a business taking an active party in the social causes, charities, and civic life of one's community and societ. Facebook founder, Mark Zuckerberg, donated $100 million to help fix schools in Newark, New Jersey. Newman's Own is a private sector company praised for its philanthropic mission since it donates all of its profits and royalties after taxes for charitable and educational purposes. However, corporate social responsibility (CSR) certainly can be more than "mere" philanthropy. The social responsibility of business can also be thought of in a broader constituency or stakeholder sense. Deskins (2011, pp. 1057-58) explains that "CSR attempts to connect corporations with public needs. By encouraging corporations to view employees, consumers, and communities in a similar manner as they do stockholder, CSR seeks to expand the role that corporations play in society." Similarly, Tyagi (2011, p. 29) states that social responsibility encompasses "…a person's obligation to consider the effects of his decisions and actions on the whole social system"; and adds that "the fundamentals of CSR management is to understand the values and principles of those who have a stake in the business operations – the stakeholders."

A constituency or stakeholder approach to corporate social responsibility requires management to balance shareholder and non-shareholder interests. Furthermore:

> Strict shareholder primacy – the idea that shareholder interests should enjoy priority over those of nonshareholders – is rejected because of the costs in can inflict on nonshareholders. For example, profit maximization, even when pursued within the boundaries of the law, can lead to plant closings that harm workers and local communities, environmental damage, and human rights violations in developing countries. Socially

responsible leadership therefore necessitates that management temper its pursuit of profit with regard for such considerations (Millon, 2011, p. 525).

Porter and Kramer (2006) take a "strategic" approach to corporate social responsibility by emphasizing shared value, that is, business making decisions that are valuable for the business but which also provide a meaningful benefit for society, such as Toyota's development of the Prius hybrid automobile. The objective is to make money, legally of course, but also benefit society by fulfilling specific societal needs or solving a societal problem, yet while reinforcing corporate strategy and goals too. Harish (2012) also takes a "strategic" as well as stakeholder approach to corporate social responsibility:

> Corporate social responsibility (CSR) is a concept whereby organizations consider the interests of society by taking responsibility for the impact of their activities on customer, suppliers, employees, shareholders, communities and other stakeholders, as well as the environment. CSR is a way firms integrate social, environmental and economic concerns into their values, culture, decision-making, strategy and operations in a transparent and accountable manner and thereby establish better practices within the firm, create wealth and improve society. CSR is certainly a strategic approach for firms to anticipate and address issues associated with their interactions and others and, through those interactions, to succeed in their business endeavors (p. 521).

The strategic implications of corporate social responsibility will be explicated further later in this work. Harsih (2012, p. 521) also adds that corporate social responsibility by purposefully including the public interest into corporate decision-making results in the "…honoring of the triple bottom line: people, planet, profit." The Business Roundtable views the corporation as an entity "chartered to serve both their shareholders and society as a whole" (Mickels, 2009, p. 274).The World Business Council for Sustainable Development explains social responsibility in a corporate context as a company's continuing commitment to act legally and morally and also to contribute to the economic development of society while improving the quality of life of their employees and their families as well as the local community and society as a whole. This definition evokes another, and even more expansive, concept of the "social responsibility" of business – "sustainability." The sustainability approach to corporate social responsibility is premised on the idea that a company must remain economically viable in the long-term, and that in order to be viable the company must take into consideration other stakeholders beyond the shareholders. Millon (2011) explains the sustainability approach to corporate social responsibility:

> as simply the realization that the corporation's long-run prosperity depends on the well-being of its various stakeholders, including workers, suppliers, and customers. Sustainability also requires ongoing availability of natural resources and a natural environment in which the corporation and its various constituencies can survive and flourish. Well-functioning markets and stable and supportive governments are also essential....The sustainability perspective sees attention to nonshareholders – including investment in their well-being – as essential to the viability and success of the firm and also to the enhancement of shareholder value....Sustainability CSR looks beyond the current quarter or year and factors in long-run benefits as a potential offset to short-term cost (pp. 530-31).

Porter and Kramer (2011) use the term "shared value" to underscore the value of sustainability and for business leaders to use a decision-making criterion in business, to wit: "Policies and operating practices that enhance the competitiveness of a company while simultaneously advancing the economic and social conditions in the communities in which it operates" (p. 66). Maggins and Tsaklanganos (2012, p. 662) reflect that there are "various definitions" of corporate social responsibility, but "...most share the theme of engaging in economically sustainable business activities that go beyond legal requirements in order to protect the well-being of employees, communities, and the environment." The objective is to simultaneously produce economic value for the company, but also value for society as a whole by helping to solve societal needs, particularly by improving the lives of the people (and potential consumers), who live in the communities where the company does business. Andre (2012) notes that corporate social responsibility is an "umbrella concept used in the fields of management, business ethics, political theory, and legal philosophy," which is used to describe the responsibilities of the corporation to constituencies beyond the shareholder group, and which "is often used interchangeably with such terms as corporate citizenship, stakeholder management, and social enterprise" (p. 134). There is thus a normative conception of social responsibility; that is, utilizing stakeholder theory to identify philosophical, ethical, and moral guidelines for the operation and management of the corporation. To wit, Hasnas (2013, p. 52) summarizes the fundamental moral implications of stakeholder theory: "Managers of an organization do not have an exclusive fiduciary duty to any one stakeholder group, but rather, are obligated to ensure that the value created by the organization is distributed among all normative shareholders and that all normative stakeholders have input into the managerial decisions that determine how the organization attempts to create that value. Normative stakeholders include the organization's financiers, employees, customers, suppliers, and local communities." Furthermore, regarding the access criterion, Hasnas (2013, p. 55) adds that "in the traditional stakeholder model of the firm, this implies that either managers must either provide a direct avenue of input for or act as a representative of the firm's employees, suppliers, customers, and local communities in deciding how the firm should act." However, for the purposes of this work, the authors are positing the concept of social responsibility as a value "above and beyond" ethics and morality since an organization may not have a moral duty based on ethics to be a "socially responsible" firm.

A corporation, of course, is a profit-making entity that exists in a competitive environment, and thus may be limited in its ability to solve a multitude of social problems particularly at the expense of the owners of the corporation – the shareholders. Where are the philanthropic guidelines for corporate contributions and improvements? How should a corporation's resources be allocated, and exactly to whom, to what extent, and in what priorities? What is the proper balance between shareholder and stakeholder interests? If a corporation unilaterally or too generously engages in social betterment, it may place itself at a disadvantage compared to other less socially responsible business entities. Being socially responsible costs money, and such efforts cut into profits. In a highly competitive market system, corporations that are too socially responsible may lessen their attractiveness to investors or simply may price themselves out of the market. "Charity begins at home." – That was the very prudent social responsibility conclusion in a *Newsweek* article (Smalley, 2007) regarding the saga of THE socially responsible firm – Ben & Jerry's, which has long been known and lauded for its civic, community, and environmental efforts. Mickels (2009, p. 274) notes that "many people consider Ben & Jerry's as the first 'socially responsible' company by introducing the concept of improving the environment as a second bottom line." Yet the company may have been *too* socially responsible and consequently neglectful of basic business concerns. Ultimately, the original former "hippies" Ben Cohen and Jerry Greenfield of Ben & Jerry's sold their interests in their company in 2000 to global consumer products giant, Unilever, which carried on the social responsibility activities of the brand to a degree; but, as *Newsweek* reported, several company franchisees, primarily small entrepreneurs, are suing the firm, contending that Ben & Jerry's treated them unfairly, for example, by not providing adequate training and assistance, by giving wholesale price "breaks" to large buyers, such as Wal-Mart and Costco, thereby undercutting them, by not sufficiently marketing their franchises, and by misrepresenting average gross sales for stores. Unilever is denying the allegations, but is working with its franchisees by waiving royalty fees, renegotiating store leases, and increasing marketing support. A representative from Unilever stated that it is an "ethic" of Ben & Jerry's to treat its franchisees well, which is all "well and good," but *Newsweek* posited that the lesson to be learned in this episode for "socially responsible" companies is that "Charity begins at home." There is a further problem in expecting the corporation to take on the betterment of the "general welfare." Corporations already possess great power, and corporate executives neither are the elected representatives of the people nor are answerable directly to the general public. Corporate executives lack the mandate that a democratic society grants to those who are supposed to promote the general welfare. Government officials, elected by the people, rightfully are thought of as the social guardians of the people.

Social responsibility, however, at least to some reasonable degree, may be in the long-term self-interest of business. "Some corporations have long supported social initiatives as a means of enhancing their own profits and long-term viability. Through charitable donations, community programs, or holistic decision-making, corporations have pursued tangible goals, such as improving workforce comfort or engendering customer goodwill, arguing that these actions align with the corporation's ultimate profit-making interests." Significantly, Munch (2012) adds that "there is some evidence that these strategies are successful" (p. 178). Wang and Qian (2012) conducted a study of the philanthropic of publicly listed Chinese firms from 2001 to 2006 and found that corporate philanthropy enhances corporate financial performance by enabling firms to elicit better stakeholder responses and to gain political resources. Tyagi (2011, p. 31) reports on studies that support the proposition that corporate social responsibility positively affects "corporate attractiveness." Afsharipour (2011), furthermore, reported on an Indian study that revealed a positive relationship between company performance and corporate social responsibility. Maggins and Tsaklanganos (2012, p. 663) report on a series of studies that indicated that "...CSR is significant in corporate decision-making because of the relationship between a firm's social policies or actions and its financial performance."

A corporation cannot long remain a viable economic entity in a society that is uneven, unstable, and deteriorating. It makes good business sense for a corporation to devote some of its resources to social betterment projects. To operate efficiently, for example, business needs educated and skilled employees. Education and training, therefore, should be of paramount interest to business leaders. A corporation, for example, can act socially responsible by providing computers to community schools and by releasing employees on company time to furnish the training. AT&T has a formal education program, which it has invested $100 million, whereby high school students "shadow" the company's workers. AT&T employees have contributed over 270,000 to the program, and more than one million students have participated in the program. British Petroleum (BP), for example, marketing itself in Europe and the U.S. as "Beyond Petroleum," before the disastrous Gulf oil spill at least, was regarded as a very socially responsible firm, especially for its environmental and alternative fuel efforts. Another illustration involves the web-search company, Google, Inc., which has committed almost one billion dollars in stock as well as a share of its profits to combat global poverty and to protect the environment (Delaney, 2005). Starbucks Corporation, in addition, has been engaged in a variety of socially responsible activities in Guatemala, such as building health clinics, and also promising to pay its coffee suppliers a premium price if they adhere to certain labor and environmental standards. The Coca-Cola company has teamed with the World Wildlife Fund to protect the arctic habitat by releasing 1.4 billion redesigned white Coke cans each showing a polar bear, which the company hopes will raise awareness of this cause. Coke made an initial donation of $2 million to the World Wildlife Fund, and Coke will match up to $1 million that Coke drinkers will be able to donate to the campaign. McDonald's is so extensively involved in charitable activities and civic affairs in local communities throughout the United States that it produces through its corporate charitable division, Ronald McDonald House Charities of South Florida, special multi-page advertising supplements to local newspapers to describe the company's many socially responsible activities – from grants, "Wish Lists," scholarships, volunteer work to, of course, the Ronald McDonald House itself.

Business also gains an improved public image by being

socially responsible. An enhanced social image should attract more customers and investors and thus provide positive benefit for the firm. Maggins and Tsaklanganos (2012, p. 661) stress social responsibility as part of a "broader concept of success" for an organization, and, accordingly, note that in 2007 64% of Fortune 100 companies published a social responsibility report which described their economic, environmental, and social performance. Afsharipour (2011) points to evidence from India that indicates that being perceived as a socially responsible firm will result in an enhanced public image and improved customer satisfaction. The organization Business for Social Responsibility conducted a survey in which 76% of consumers stated would switch to retailers associated with good causes, 76% states they would switch to brands associated with good causes, and 59% of consumers believed that business should help address community problems (Forman, 1996). *Business Week* (Marketing, 2012) recently provided examples of companies engaging in socially responsible marketing as one way to persuade consumers to spend in a difficult economy, to wit: Sketchers USA launched a brand called BOBS, meaning Benefiting Others By Shoes, which results in the company donating two pairs of shoes for every one sold; Urban Outfitters features clothes by Threads for Thought, which gives part of its sales proceeds to humanitarian groups; Nordstrom sells hats made by Krochet Kids International, which enlists impoverished people in Uganda and Peru, for example, to make hats which are sold in the U.S. for $24; and Feed Projects, which makes T-shirts, handbags, and accessories, donates a percentage of its profits to United Nations anti-hunger programs. *Business Week* (Marketing, 2012, p. 1) emphasized that when implemented correctly, these socially responsible retailing efforts are good strategies that "do good and make donors feel good too," especially young consumers who may not have the means to make large charitable contributions but who admire brands that are "trendy" but which also reflect a save-the-planet theme. Another example of actively doing social "good" based on a philanthropic definition of "social responsibility" was very nicely "captured" in the title of a *Wall Street Journal* article describing the social responsibility efforts of the Internet search company, Google. The very apt title to the article was "Google: From 'Don't Be Evil' to

How to Do Good" (Delaney, 2008). The article related that Google in 2008 announced a major philanthropic venture by which the company will contribute $30 million in grants and investments to a variety of charitable as well as for-profit organizations. Google's civic efforts encompass providing money to predict and prevent diseases, to develop solar power, empower the poor with information regarding public services, and to create jobs by investing in small- and medium-sized businesses throughout the "developing" world in order to boost employment. The essence of the *Wall Street Journal* article was that Google has "graduated" from being a company that "only" refrained from committing harm to a company now actively and substantially engaged in making socially responsible contributions throughout the world, thereby materially enhancing the company's reputation. To further illustrate, the Walt Disney Company, in an effort to portray a socially responsible message, as well as to attract customers to its theme parks, commenced a program, called "Give a Day, Get a Disney Day," whereby the company will give away a million one-day, one-park tickets to people who volunteer at select charities. A corporation that acts more socially responsible not only secures public favor, but also avoids public disfavor. To illustrate, for many years the large multi-national pharmaceutical companies were criticized for not providing AIDS drugs for free or at greatly reduced prices to African governments. In response to public criticism, the pharmaceutical responded in a socially responsible (and also egoistic manner) by giving the drugs away or selling them at cost. Moreover, certain pharmaceutical companies, such as Roche and GlaxoSmithKline, on their social responsibility and sustainability websites have statements indicating preferential pricing and accessibility as well as limited patent policies for AIDs drugs going to African and other less developed countries (Roche, 2007; GlaxoSmithKline, 2005). Furthermore, these policies have now been extended to states in the United States to provide the drugs to poor patients by means of "Patient Assistance Programs" (Tasker, 2011; Tasker, 2010). Accordingly, social responsibility and also good public relations are achieved. In response to criticism from the Humane Society, the International House of Pancakes (IHOP) now has a social responsibility website that states it is against the cruel treatment of animals, its eggs are "cruelty free," and that the animals used for its food receive "dignified humane treatment." Wal-Mart, the giant retailer, in response to criticisms from environmentalists and labor activists, now has a director of global ethics, who will be responsible for developing and enforcing company standards of conduct, as well as a "senior director for stakeholder engagement," whose role will be to develop a new model of business engagement that produces value for society. Similarly, clothing and apparel manufacturers, such as Nike and the Gap, in response to criticism by labor and consumer groups about exploitive working conditions in overseas "sweatshops," have ended abusive working conditions and now report on their social responsibility efforts and achievements overseas.   The NBC television network will accept liquor advertisements but, out of a concern of criticism from government regulators and health advocates, only if the advertisements carry a "socially responsible" message, such as urging viewers who drink to have a "designated driver."

Business is part of society and subject to society's mandates; and if society wants more "responsibility" from business, business cannot ignore this "request" without the risk of incurring society's anger, perhaps in the form of consumer boycotts, higher taxes, or more onerous government regulation. Lindgreen, Maon, Reast, and Yani-De-Soriano (2012) emphasize that: "Beyond the moral arguments and value-based debates that characterize the complex landscapes of CSR-related concepts and ideas…, corporate commitment to socially responsible management practices is associated with a conviction that the failure to meet basic social rules or expectations pertaining to the way organizations behave can result in perceptions of those organizations as illegitimate…" (p. 393). This perception can be particularly evident in organizations that are deemed to be "controversial industry sectors," such as tobacco, alcohol, gambling, weapons, and adult entertainment, as well as organizations that have environmental or social "ethical issues," such as the nuclear, oil, and bio-tech industries (Lindgreen, Maon, Reast, and Yani-De-Soriano, 2012, p. 393). Regarding controversial industries, De Roeck and Delobbe (2012) found that corporate social responsibility also improves employee relationships.

Over a decade ago, a *Business Week/Harris* poll (Taylor, 2011; Editorials, *Business Week*, 2000) found that only 4% of the public believed that the sole purpose of corporations is to make profits for shareholders; rather, some 95% believed that corporations should sometimes sacrifice some profit do more for employees, communities, and society. Sir John Brown, former chief executive officer of BP, astutely comprehended that society wants and expects business to be socially responsible, and that to be so is in the long-term self-interest of BP and business. Then, BP stood for not only "British Petroleum" but also "Beyond Petroleum" for all the alternative energy and social responsibility efforts that the company was engaging in under his stewardship. Maggins and Tsaklanganos (2012, p. 663) state that "socially responsible activities may also improve a firms' standing in the eyes of external stakeholders such as bankers, suppliers, creditors, investors, and government officials, which may bring about economic benefits." As such, an egoist and rational actor will surely see the instrumental value of a prudent degree of social responsibility in today's global business marketplace.

Obviously, superior product and service quality and competitive pricing are essential for business success. Yet another strategic factor to success has emerged in the present business environment – social responsibility. The idea is not "only" to make profits but then to "give back" to the community by means of civil, social, and environmental efforts. Yet a strategic approach to social responsibility would combine profits and social activism; that is, the smart and social company will deliver products and services that naturally are profitable but that also serve society by, for example, by saving energy and improving the environment. The idea for a strategic business approach is to incorporate the value of social responsibility into the firm's business model. Such an approach will enhance opportunities, increase profits, and expand the firm's market share. In essence, the ultimate goal is not only to contribute in a socially responsible manner to the community but to bring new socially responsible products and services into the marketplace. That degree of social responsibility is the egoistic business model for today's astute business leaders. Exxon-Mobil for example, recently launched a social responsibility campaign to build schools in Angola, which (perhaps not coincidentally) is an emerging oil power. Coca-Cola Co. is very extensively involved in providing clear drinking water to the "developing world," for example, by furnishing water purification systems and lessons to local communities. This meritorious social responsibility effort is designed also to promote "Coke's" reputation as a global diplomat and local benefactor. "Coke," by the way, uses a great deal of water in producing its products.

Another example of "smart," strategic, social responsibility is Microsoft's "wellness" efforts to help its overweight employees. The company, which already provides free medical coverage to its employees, now has created a weight management benefit for employees. The software company will pay for 80% of the cost, up to $6000, for a comprehensive, clinical, weight loss program for employees. The program, intended for employees who are obese or clinically overweight, includes up to a year's worth of sessions with a personal trainer, behavioral and nutritional counseling, support groups, and medical supervision. Microsoft in the long-run expects to obtain a return on its health care investment for the formerly obese and overweight employees due to cost savings from less prescription drugs and fewer doctor and hospital visits. Similarly, Johnson & Johnson has invested substantially in employee health through its Wellness & Prevention program; but the company has received an excellent return-on-investment, because the program has been estimated by the company to have saved $250 million in employee health care costs over the past decade, with the savings representing a return of $2.71 for every dollar spent (Million, 2011, p. 532). Millon (2011) concludes that "the whole point is to generate net gains in the future from expenditures incurred in the present – benefits to nonshareholders come not at the expensed of shareholders but rather are deployed for their ultimate advantage" (p. 533). Millon (2011) labels this corporate social responsibility approach "strategic" (p. 533).

HR Magazine in a human resources context underscored the egoistic and strategic rationale for a company to be rightly perceived as a socially responsible one. In a constrained and highly competitive global labor market, the shrewd corporate executive will use his or her firm's social responsibility stance to attract new employees, especially top talent, as well as to engage and retain highly skilled and highly motivated current employees (Fox, 2007). To bolster its argument, *HR Magazine* (Fox, 2007) pointed to a 2003 survey where 70% of North American students surveyed stated that they would not even apply for a job in a company that was deemed "socially irresponsible." Clark and Babson (2012, pp. 819-20) emphasize the consumer rationale for corporate social responsibility:

> Approximately 68 million U.S. consumers have stated a preference for making purchasing decisions based upon their sense of social and environmental responsibility. Some consumers use their purchasing power to punish companies for negative corporate behavior, and many other consumers use their purchasing power to reward companies that positively address a social or environmental issue. Current surveys have shown that forty-nine percent of Americans have boycotted companies whose behavior they perceive is not in the best interest of society. Meanwhile, recent research has also indicated that where price and quality are equal, eighty-seven percent of consumers would switch from their current brand to a brand that is socially responsible (pp. 819-20).

Tyagi (2011, p. 31) reports on a global survey of over 1000 corporate executives conducted by the *Economist* which indicated that executives perceived business benefits of corporate social responsibility because CSR "…increases attractiveness to potential and existing employees." Afsharipour (2011) relates the comments of high-level executives of Indian companies who believe that companies with corporate social responsibility programs, particularly employee-driven ones, will increase employee pride, satisfaction, loyalty, retention, and productivity.

Professor Imran Ali (Personal Communication with Bahaudin Mujtaba, 2013) of the COMSTATS Institute of Information Technology in Lahore, Pakistan, conducted a study on how corporate social responsibility and corporate reputation influence employee engagement. The study was based on primary data which had been collected from various banking sector organizations of Pakistan. The unit of analysis of the study was the individual employees; and therefore the target population in the study was the employees working in various banks in different cities of Pakistan. A total of 400 survey questionnaires was distributed, out of which 284 were returned back, leaving 71 % response rate, which is quite acceptable in social sciences. The survey was personally administered in order to maximize the response rate. The sample population included employees of diverse demographic profile. It included people from public/private, national/multi-national banks, age groups, income levels, educational backgrounds, as well as belonging from various functional departments, in order to generalize the findings of the study. The key findings were that the higher the level of corporate social responsibility activities the higher the reputation of the corporation and thus the higher the level of employee engagement (Ali, 2013; Ali, Rehman and Akram, 2011).

The study was conducted to investigate the potential influence of corporate social responsibility and corporate reputation on employee engagement. The study found a significant influence of corporate social responsibility on corporate reputation and building higher levels of employee engagement. Similarly it found that corporations with higher level of reputation of doing well also enjoy a higher level of employee engagement. Academically, the study had a number of implications. This study suggested that employees conceptualize CSR on different perspectives, such as how well the organization communicate with its environment and how ethically it provides benefit to its stakeholders through its products and services. The companies with higher levels of CSR interventions and reputations of doing well can attract committed employees who engage themselves with their work and exhibit cooperation as well.

The study, therefore, proposed multiple recommendations to various stakeholders. For corporations, the study recommended to increase the amount of CSR activities to enhance organizations' reputational capital. A high corporate reputation of doing "good" can benefit the organization in many ways; it will help organizations attract and retain customers, investors and, of course, employees. The employees who work in organizations having the reputation of doing "good" through the CSR exhibit higher level of motivation and commitment to perform better for organizational success. Corporations can also use CSR and that concomitant high reputation of doing "good" to survive any economic downturn. For managers, the study recommended that they involve employees in CSR activities, for example, through voluntary activities for community betterment, so that they may feel a sense of accomplishment and "belonging" to the organization. The manager should also communicate CSR activities done by the organization to employees in order to achieve higher levels of employee engagement. Finally, for business owners, the study recommends that CSR should not be considered as an expense; rather it should be considered as an investment that provides higher yields in the form of higher customer loyalty and employee engagement. Therefore, business owners should utilize considerable resources for CSR to build a high reputation of doing "good" so as to achieve better organizational outcomes.

Similarly, but from the employee and job applicant perspective, Babson and Clark (2012) relate that:

> Consumers not only prefer to purchase from but also to work for, companies who are committed to social and environmental issues. More than two-thirds of employees (sixty-nine percent) consider the social and environmental track record of the company in deciding where to work. This preference is especially strong among Masters of Business Administration ("MBA") graduates, who overwhelmingly (eighty-eight percent) have said that would be comfortable taking a pay cut to work for a company that has ethical business practices versus one that does not (p. 821).

Christopher and Bernhart (2009) report on studies that demonstrated the recruitment and retention benefits of social responsibility, for example, a study indicating that 64% of employees indicated that corporate social responsibility (CSR) activities increased their loyalty, and that 90% of employees would choose an employer viewed as more socially responsible. Christopher and Bernhart (2007) also report that a "meta-analysis of over 50 studies found CSR social components, including treatment of employees, significantly affected financial performance measures. In addition, 'objective CSR performance ratings were significant predictors of employer attractiveness to potential applicants" (p. 9). Also in the HR context, Tyagi, 2011, p. 32) explains the benefits of a company being a socially responsible one: "Employees are likely to identify with socially responsible companies, especially when company values match an employee's self-identity....Employees can feel proud to belong to and work for a company that is acknowledged for its positive contribution to society....CSR can enhance positive workplace attitudes, such as job satisfaction." Udgata and Das (2012, p. 52) add that "from a human resources perspective, the ability to attract top talent is a major challenge for companies. But the best and brightest today are looking for more than impressive salaries and stock prices. They want something more – something that gives meaning to their work and their lives. Supporting social entrepreneurs in different ways shows that companies care about more than the "bottom line." Accordingly, corporate social responsibility can be a key recruitment and retention strategy for the global organization, which business leaders and managers can use to attract, develop, and keep a highly engaged, motivated, and productive workforce.

However, a socially responsible firm must also be a realistic; that is, socially responsible and environmental efforts must be sustainable economically and should have some relationship to the firm's business. Employees should also be engaged directly in the company's social responsibility activities so as to engage them, inspire them, motivate them, and thereby enhance morale and productivity. Moreover, a firm's social responsibility program does not have to be a multi-million dollar effort; rather, something as simple as an employee social responsibility "suggestion box" or as straightforward as a recycling or energy saving program will do to promote employee involvement as well as to promote and give credence to employee social values. Nonetheless, despite the size, a firm's social responsibility efforts should be publicized widely within the company, for example, in company newsletters, as well as externally, for example in company annual "social responsibility" reports. Being socially responsible, therefore, advises *HR Magazine*, is a smart and sustainable business strategy, especially in a human resource context. An actual illustration of *HR Magazine's* social responsibility recommendation is the PepsiCo. The company's chairperson and CEO, Indra Nooyi, has urged companies to follow her company's approach to being a "good" global company; and by "good" she means that in addition to having a strong financial performance, a firm must value and take care of its employees and also the public's health and the environment. For example, PepsiCo has expanded its product lines to include more juices and waters as well as introducing low-sugar versions of its popular "fitness drink," Gatorade. The company is also promoting energy management, for example, by reducing its water usage and creating more environmentally "friendly" packaging. One major benefit of being a socially responsible firm, PepsiCo has discovered, is that its employees are inspired and energized, thereby helping the company to retain employees.

Business Week published a very revealing Social Responsibility Special Report that enumerated and extolled the socially responsible practices of many companies today; and then asked the seminal question as to whether these laudatory socially responsible efforts positively contributed to the companies' "bottom-line" (Engardio, 2007). *Business Week* listed these companies in a chart, grouped by sectors of the economy, and then detailed their social responsibility as well as "eco-friendly" activities, and under a very revealing chart sub-title, "Who's Doing Well by Doing Good." For example, Unilever, the British-Dutch multinational, has opened a free community laundry in Sal Paulo, Brazil, provides financing to help tomato growing farmers to convert to more environmentally sensitive irrigation systems, and has funded a floating hospital that provides free medical care to people in Bangladesh. In Ghana, Unilever provides safe drinking water to communities; and in India, the company's employees assist women in isolated villages commence small entrepreneurial enterprises. As related by *Business Week*, Unilever CEO, Patrick Cescau, views the company's social responsibility effort as one of its biggest strategic challenges for the

21st century. Cescau explains that since 40% of the company's sales come from consumers in developing countries, assisting these countries to overcome poverty and to safeguard the environment is vital to the company's sustaining its competitive advantage. In order for the company to maintain its leadership role, it must be concerned about the impact its policies have on society, local communities, the environment, as well as future generations. Cescau's rationale for social responsibility underscores the ethically egoistic justification that "good deeds" will produce strategic and competitive advantages and thus inure to the benefit of the company in the long-term. Another example given by *Business Week* was General Electric, which is taking the lead in developing wind power and hybrid engines. Even Wal-Mart, perennially criticized by labor and human rights groups, was praised for its efforts to save energy and to purchase more electricity derived from renewable sources. GlaxoSmithKline was given credit for investing in poor nations to develop drugs. Moreover, the company was praised for being one of the first major pharmaceutical companies to sell AIDS drugs at cost in 100 countries worldwide. *Business Week* pointed out that such socially responsible behavior by the large pharmaceutical company worked in its favor as the company is working much more effectively with these governments to make sure its patents are protected. In addition, as noted in *Business Week*, the company's CEO, Jean-Pierre Garner, explained that the company's social responsibility efforts produce other egoistic advantages, such as motivating top scientists to work for the firm, as well as enhancing the overall morale of the company's workforce, which gives the company, stated Garner, a competitive advantage. Another example was Dow Chemical, which is developing and investing in solar power and water treatment technologies. Also, Dow CEO, Andrew N. Liveris, explained that there is a "100% overlap" between the company's business values and its social and environmental values. Toyota was cited as another illustration of a socially responsible firm due to its work with hybrid gas-electric cars. Such practices have given Toyota a very good reputation as a company that makes clean-running and fuel efficient vehicles; and *Business Week* (Engardio, 2007) related that this "green" reputation has given Toyota a competitive edge. Another example involves

PepsiCo and its charitable-giving program, called Refresh, where Pepsi drinkers can vote online, using votes obtained from the company's products, for "refreshing ideas that change the world" (Bauerlein, 2011). Winners will have their socially responsible projects funded by the company. Past winners of grants have included cheerleading squads for the disabled students, a project to make school bus windshields more aerodynamic. The Refresh program has been extensively advertised by the company in order to give consumers a "voice" in the company's charitable giving, and also, significantly, to engage consumers, enhance the company's image and brand as a socially responsible one, and in the long-term to increase sales and profits. Business "sustainability" and success emerge as the very practical instrumental reasons given by the companies for their social responsibility efforts. Furthermore, social responsibility is certainly not just a concept applied in the United States; rather, U.S. multinationals doing business overseas as well as foreign companies in their own countries are now actively engaged today in social responsibility activities.

Chapter 6

Corporate Social Responsibility: Global Perspectives[2]

The topic of social responsibility has emerged as such a critical one for global business too. To illustrate, Hai-yan and Silva (2012) state that "the internationalization of business, the opening of markets and the trend towards globalization means that corporate social responsibility (CSR) has become a concept of great interest and study in recent years" (p. 57). Afsharipour (2011) relates that corporate social responsibility (CSR) "...debates are not just occurring in developed economies. Countries around the world are engaging in rich and nuanced debates, and undertaking significant reforms in the corporate governance and CSR arenas" (p. 996). Mickels (2009) adds that "directors all over the world are questioning whether corporations should exist solely to maximize shareholder profit" (p. 271). Harish (2012) concurs that corporate social responsibility is a "globally applicable concept" but advises that "...its interpretation will vary from country to country, industry to industry and company to company because of differing local situations and differing demands of stakeholders in different locations and industries" (p. 526).

The prevalence of corporate social responsibility (CSR) on a global basis has been illustrated by a survey conducted by the Society of Human Resource Management (SHRM) in 2007 (Workplace Visions, 2007). SHRM found that a majority of Human Resource professionals in the countries surveyed (United States, Australia, India, China, Canada, Mexico, and Brazil) reported that their

---

[2] Coauthored with Bahaudin G. Mujtaba, Nova Southeastern University.

organizations had corporate social responsibility practices in place. SHRM put forth a number of reasons for the extent of corporate social responsibility. First, companies realize that they need to respond to large scale social problems before they become a threat to business. Second, on a more positive note, SHRM contends that solutions to major social problems can increasingly be viewed as new sources of business opportunities. That is, providing goods and services to the people of developing nations may be a way to enter into potentially vast markets of consumers. Similarly, "going green" and investing in environmentally "friendly" technology may be a way for companies to initially establish themselves in potentially highly profitable energy sectors. Two illustrations related by SHRM would be the success of Toyota with the hybrid car, and Nokia's and Ericsson's efforts to bring mobile communications technology to the developing world. Corporate social responsibility, SHRM thus concludes, is an active and essential component of creating competitive advantage and thereby promoting value creation for the firm and its stakeholders. Another example would be the Coca-Cola's company's efforts to provide clean water to parts of the developing world, which Coke also hopes to promote goodwill, boost local economies, and broaden its customer base. Royal Caribbean Cruise Company is teaming up with a Haitian non-profit organization to build a primary school, which is located on land the company leases from the government as a stop for its ships in the port town of Labadee. Wal-Mart is now selling online handicrafts made by women artisans in developing countries, such as dresses made in Kenya and jewelry from Guatemala and Thailand. Over 500 items from 20,000 female artisans will be offered for sale, which certainly will help the female artisans but also improve the company's global image. Millon (2011) calls for a "sustainability" approach to corporate social responsibility globally: "For transnational corporations doing business in developed countries, sustainability may require investment in community-level infrastructure development projects, technological innovation, education, and health care. As these investments lead to greater productivity and better product quality, workers and producers can earn higher incomes, allowing the local population to enjoy a higher standard of living" (p. 531). Two excellent examples of global "sustainable" CSR are: 1) The Norwegian company, Yara International, the world's largest chemical fertilizer company, has sponsored public/private partnerships to develop storage, transportation, and port facilities in parts of Africa with significant untapped agricultural potential, thereby developing local agriculture, providing jobs and improved incomes for farmers, and at the same time benefiting the company through an increased demand for its fertilizer products. 2) The Nestle Company is working to improve milk production in certain regions of India, by investing in well drilling, refrigeration, veterinary medicine, and training, thereby significantly increasing output and enhancing product quality, certainly beneficial to the company, and at the same time allowing the company to pay higher prices for farmers and their employees, resulting in a higher standard of living for the local community.

The United Nations now has a business initiative on corporate social responsibility, called the United Nations Global Compact, whereby companies can join and thus voluntarily agree to make improvements in human rights, labor, the environment, and combating corruption. The World Bank, moreover, now has an Internet course on social responsibility, called "CSR and Sustainable Competitiveness," offered by its educational and training division, the World Bank Institute. The corporate social responsibility course is designed for "high-level" private sector managers, government officials and regulators, practitioners, academics, and journalists. One major purpose to the course is to provide a "conceptual framework" for improving the business environment to support social responsibility efforts and practices by corporations and business. The course is also designed to assist companies to formulate a social responsibility strategy based on "integrity and sound values" as well as one with a long-term perspective. By being socially responsible, declares the World Bank, businesses not only will accrue benefits, but also civil society as a whole will benefit from the "positive contributions" of business to society. Although it is beyond the scope of this book to discuss in detail the World Bank's very laudable CSR educational effort, a few key elements in the course must be addressed. First and foremost, as the World Bank points out, correctly so, there is no single, commonly accepted, definition of the critical term "CSR." Nonetheless, the World Bank offers its definition, stating that CSR generally refers to: 1) "a collection of policies and practices linked to the relationship with key stakeholders, values, compliance with legal requirements, and respect for people, communities and the environment; and 2) the commitment of business to contribute to sustainable development." The World Bank also explains the key term "Corporate Citizenship," which is "the concept of the corporation as a citizen" and which is a term often used when referring to CSR. As a matter of fact, the World Bank notes, again quite correctly, that the terms "CSR" and "Corporate Citizenship" are at times used interchangeably. The World Bank, moreover, in order to fully explicate CSR, indicates several material components to that concept, to wit: 1) environmental protection, 2) labor security, 3) human rights, 4) community involvement, 5) business standards, 6) marketplace, 7) enterprise and economic development, 8) health protection, 9) education and leadership development, and 10) human disaster relief. The World Bank also offers several decision-making frameworks for companies to plan, implement, and measure CSR. An important part of the World Bank course is a segment, eminently practical for business, called "Benefits of CSR." There are, according to the World Bank, many reasons why it pays for companies, both large businesses and small and medium enterprises to be socially responsible and thus to be conscious about the interests and values of key stakeholders. The World Bank pointed to a survey conducted by its Institute that indicated that 52% of its respondents had either "rewarded" or "punished" businesses by either buying or not buying their products based on the perceived social responsibility performance of the companies. Other reasons for being a socially responsible firm are, according to the Bank, as follows: 1) obtaining a "social license" to operate from key stakeholders; 2) ensuring "sustainable competitiveness," 3) creating new business opportunities, 4) attracting and retaining quality investors and business partners, 5) securing cooperation from local communities, 6) avoiding difficulties due to socially irresponsible behavior, 7) obtaining government support, and 8) building "political capital." These reasons make the "business case" for being a socially responsible company.

Corporate social responsibility is being promoted in the European Community. France in 2001 was the first country to require systematic disclosures of the social and environmental performance of major corporations; and England now also requires disclosures by corporations of their social performance. In 2000, the European Council in Lisbon formally encouraged companies to become more socially responsible, for example, by taking into consideration sustainable development. Moreover, "the European Commission has recognized that shareholder value is not achieved merely through maximizing short-term profits, but also through 'market-oriented yet responsible behavior'" (Mickels, 2009, p. 277). Furthermore, Mickels (2009, p. 276) reports that in 2006, the European Commission enacted a Resolution, titled "Corporation Social Responsibility: A New Partnership," which proclaimed that corporate social responsibility has become an increasingly important topic for the European Community and that CSR is in integral "part of the debate about globalization, competitiveness, and sustainability." Mickels (2009, pp. 276-77) explains that "according to the European Commission, CSR is 'a concept whereby companies integrate social and environmental concerns in their business operations and in their interaction with their stakeholders on a voluntary basis.'" However, both the British and American definitions of corporate social responsibility are "vague"; but nevertheless, "...both embody a conviction that a corporation's existence should not relate solely to making money for the sake of making money but that a corporation has a social responsibility to contribute and improve the community in which it operates" (Mickels, 2009, p. 277).

In China, Hai-yan and Silva (2012) relate that due to the scandals regarding product safety and environmental damage as well as a concern over workers' rights, the concept of corporate social responsibility is developing as an issue for Chinese companies and their executives. Hai-yan and Silva (2012, pp. 61-62) conducted a survey of the executives of 206 companies, mainly engaging in trade, in the Beijing area, and they found an awareness of social responsibility among the executives, and specifically found that these executives believed that a company could best be a socially responsible one by complying with the law, providing customers with safe and reliable products, improving the quality of the education system in China, and protecting the environment. Hai-yan and Silva (2012) cite egoistic "market" reasons for this development of corporate social responsibility internationally as well as now encompassing China: "…We have seen the expansion of the concept of CSR from large to small and medium enterprises as well as an increase in corporate awareness, knowing that their performance in the market depends on the market demands, the society in which they operate, and the socially responsible actions which they perform" (p. 58). To further make the point, a survey conducted by Cone Communications and Echo Research (Chu, 2012) of more than 10,000 consumers in 10 countries found that three out of four respondents in China stated that they were very likely to change brands to those associated with a good cause (assuming there was an alternative in the same price range and of similar quality). Furthermore, 83% of the respondents in China stated that they refused to purchase a company's product when they became aware that the company acted in an irresponsible manner.

India emerges as a country in the vanguard of corporate social responsibility developments – both legally as well as practically. Regarding India and corporate social responsibility (CSR), Afsharipour (2011) relates that:

> Over the past several decades, India began a shift from the philanthropic model of social responsibility that predominated the era before liberalization, to a more Milton Friedman-style approach that focuses on the shareholders, and finally to the currently popular stakeholder model of CSR. The stakeholder model of CSR recognizes that companies have responsibilities to not only their shareholders, but also to their employees, customers, surrounding communities (including the environment) and society as a whole…According to a broad survey of Indian executives, many Indian firms have a sense of a social mission and purpose. These executives do not see shareholder wealth maximization as their primary goal. Instead, 'they take pride in enterprise

success-but also in family prosperity, regional advancement, and national renaissance' (p. 1014).

Harish (2012) lists in detail the social responsibility activities of several multinational as well as Indian companies in India. Examples include Bajaj Auto, which has created a Trust to help promote development among the rural poor so as to raise rural living standards; Infosys Technologies, Ltd, which has a Foundation to support and promote underprivileged sections of society, such as training poor women in tailoring and donating sewing machines; and the Indian Oil Company, which has adopted as part of its strategic plans several environmental initiatives, especially the development of cleaner fuels. The India government, in addition, is now involved legally in corporate social responsibility. In 2009 the Indian government, specifically the Ministry of Corporate Affairs (MCA), promulgated Voluntary Guidelines for Corporate Social Responsibility. The Guidelines, relates Afsharipour (2011), are premised on a "fundamental principle," to wit: "Each business entity should formulate a CSR policy to guide its strategic planning and provide a roadmap for its CSR initiatives, and that should be an integral part of overall business policy and aligned with a company's business goals. The policy should be framed with the participation of various level executives and should be approved and overseen by the board" (p. 1019). Moreover, "according to the CSR Guidelines, the CSR policy should cover the following core elements: (i) care for all stakeholders, including shareholders, employees, customers, suppliers, project-affected people, society at large...; (ii) ethical functioning, transparency, and accountability; (iii) respect for workers' rights and welfare; (iv) respect for the environment; and (vi) activities for social and inclusive development" (p. 1019). These Guidelines, Afsharipour (2011) further explains:

> attempt to move beyond a philanthropic model of CSR to a more expansive view of CSR that envisions the integration of social and environmental issues into businesses' decisions goals, and operations, and in interactions between corporations and their

> stakeholders....India's CSR Guidelines, along with the
> government's various public statements, view directors
> from a Gandhian perspective as trustees with duties to
> shareholders, stakeholders, and society as a whole (pp.
> 997-98).

Also, in India, in 2009, the government mandated that public-sector oil companies spend 2% of their net profits on corporate social responsibility efforts; and there are proposals for the government to mandate that private sector companies spend 2% to 5% of their net profits on corporate social responsibility efforts. However, in 2010, the Indian government "just" required that Indian companies have a CRS policy which "targets" a 2% spending allocation on CSR; and that companies provide disclosure and details of their CSR efforts and suitable reasons for these efforts (or the lack thereof) in an annual report (Afsharipour, 2011). Afsharipour (2011) criticizes the 2009 Indian law because "the CSR Guidelines...provide little concrete guidance on how companies are to implement the guidelines or what legal changes need to be made to ensure that socially responsible practices will be part of a firm's way of doing business" (p. 1019). Afsharipour (2011), moreover, criticizes the 2010 law because "the recommendations do not explain in any detail what constitutes CSR" (p. 1021). However, Afsharipour (2011) does admit that "one important aspect of the CSR Guidelines is the move toward additional disclosure. Very few Indian companies disclose their CSR policies, so additional disclosure could be a tool NGO advocates and lawyers to work with companies and pressure them to comply with their CSR policies" (p. 1022). As such, in order to assist companies fulfill their social responsibility obligations, Kumar, Kuberudu, and Krishna (2011, pp. 10-11) offer the following recommendations for "socially responsible" businesses in, as well as doing business in, India: 1) create and nurture an "eco-friendly environment" within and outside the organization; 2) adopt poor, needy, and "sleepy" villages and bring them into inclusive growth by supplying "econ friendly" projects; 3) wage a "war" on bribery and corruption; 4) control pollution, including "social pollution," and help build a "healthy society"; 5) provide assistance when natural calamities occur; 6) develop the "highest ethical standards" with "transparency" as the "watch word"; 7) avoid deceptive and exaggerated advertisement, be restrained by "general social acceptability" regarding advertising, and do not exploit women in advertising; 8) offer financial scholarships and financial assistance to meritorious students; assistance in education and vocational training; and adopt schools, providing for their growth and management. These social responsibility activities will naturally help Indian companies fulfill their legal obligations, but also will result in a more stable society, the survival of the organization, and its maximization of profits, since there is a "direct relation" between the well-being of the organization and the good will of the people in society (Kumar, Kuberudu, and Krishna, 2011, p. 8). Actually, the Society for Human Resource Management (McConnell, 2006) reported on a global corporate social responsibility survey of human resource professionals from the U.S., Australia, China, and India that indicated that the respondents from India, who were surveyed before the recent Indian CSR laws, were more likely to have formal corporate social responsibility policies, such as written objectives and reports, or corporate social responsibility efforts tied to the organization's mission and/or goals. Of course, there is a big difference between India and a country such as the United States, because in India corporate social responsibility is now legally mandated to some degree by the government, whereas in the U.S. a company *may* be socially responsible pursuant to corporate constituency statutes and also *may* impose a legal obligation upon itself to be socially responsible by forming a social benefit corporation; but neither the federal government nor the state governments in the U.S. presently are mandating legally that companies be socially responsible ones.

Chapter 7

Socially Responsible Investing

The social responsibility of business has been heightened by the creation of social responsibility investment funds for the socially responsible investor (SRI). Clark and Babson (2012, p. 819) indicate that "accelerating consumer and investor demand has resulted in the formation of a substantial marketplace for companies that are using the power of business to solve social problems." Haymore (2011, pp. 1337-38) points out that "unlike traditional investors, SRIs seek to maximize a balance of financial return and social good. SRIs express their values on issues like social justice and the environment through investing in companies that they believe will have a positive social impact. They expect that companies will consider the impact business decisions will have on constituencies like employees, communities, and the environment." As such, there exist today several "socially responsible" investment firms to ensure investors they are investing in not only financially prudent companies, but also socially responsible ones. These funds promise to invest the participants' money only in companies that are ethical, moral, and socially responsible. Naturally, investors want to invest in quality companies whose business will make a profit for the shareholder-investors; yet socially responsible investors want to invest in such companies only if they also are sensitive to the needs of other stakeholders, and conduct business in a socially responsible as well as an environmentally responsible manner. *Business Week* reported in 2005 (Pressman, 2005) that socially responsible funds possessed assets of over $34 billion. *Business Week* (Engardio, 2007) also reported that the assets of mutual fund companies that invest in firms meeting social responsibility criteria have increased dramatically from $12 billion in 1995 to $178 billion in 2005. Sadler (2010, p. 204) reported that as of 2007 there were 260 "socially screened" mutual fund products in the United States with assets of $201 billion. Cummings (2012) reports that in 2007 there was more than $2.7 trillion, representing about 11% of all assets under professional management in the United States, that were invested in "portfolios screened for social responsibility" (p. 583). Clark and Babson (2012, p. 822) reported that socially responsible investing (SRI) has increased over the past thirty years to account for almost 10% of U.S. assets under financial management, which was approximately $2.3 trillion in socially responsible investments. Clark and Babson (2012, p. 822) also indicate that a 2010 J.P. Morgan report, called "Impact Investment: An Emerging Asset Class," estimated the size of the socially responsible market opportunity to be between $400 billion and $1 trillion. As such, Clark and Babson (2012, p. 222) conclude that "SRI has evolved in both public and private markets, becoming an institutionalized sector of the professional asset management market and giving rise to a distinct venture capital and private equity industry of funds and individual investors seeking value-aligned investment opportunities."

A key issue in socially responsible investing, of course, is the performance of these funds. Pressman (2005), in *Business Week*, noted that "investors don't necessarily surrender anything in performance to pursue nobler goals, but individual fund returns do vary...." (p. 124). *Business Week* also provided a comparative table of performance of social responsibility funds (Pressman, p. 125).Today, many more socially responsible funds exist, including mutual funds; and the socially-minded investor has a wide choice of funds, ranging from those that stress environmental causes and workers' rights, to those that reflect ethical and religious value as well as civic and charitable activities. Accordingly, if one is interested in developing a portfolio with social responsibility concerns, *McClatchy-Tribune News* (2011) refers the discerning socially responsible investor to the following websites:

- Bankrate.com – providing an overview of socially responsible investing, investment areas and how to become a socially responsible investor.
- CFA Institute at cfainstitute.org – providing recommendations for socially responsible investing, including establishing goals and objectives and investigating investment funds.
- Investopedia at investopedia.com – providing descriptions of socially responsible investing and supplying links to other pertinent topics.
- TIAA-CREF at tiaa-cref.org – providing strategies for socially responsible investing.

Dow Jones, moreover, has a Sustainability Index, which tracks the financial performance of companies which are regarded as "…leaders in embracing opportunities and managing risks deriving from economic, environmental and social developments" (Sadler, 2010, p. 204). Dow Jones did this, Sadler (2010, p. 204) relates, because "…sustainability is a catalyst for enlightened and disciplined management, and, thus, a crucial success factor." Furthermore, many companies today have their own social responsibility websites that extol their corporate social responsibility efforts (CSR) in the form of CSR, social performance, sustainability, or values reports (Hemlock, 2007). Furthermore, certain mutual funds identify socially responsible businesses. Moreover, social responsibility stock indexes exist, such, as noted, the Dow Jones World Sustainability index as well as the Financial Times Stock Exchange's FTSE4Good index, the Global Impact Investing Rating System, *Fortune* magazine, and the World Bank, have measures of social responsibility among the criteria used to evaluate and rank corporations. Similarly, *Business Week* magazine for several years has issued special reports, rankings, and descriptions of corporate philanthropy and social responsibility.. Moreover, *Business Week* also noted that a growing investor demand for more accurate information on the relationship between social responsibility and profits has resulted in increased research. For example, one company, called Innovest, in addition to measuring firms' performance by means of conventional financial criteria, studies a variety of different factors, such as employee practices and energy use. The problem, of course, is that ascertaining the financial consequences of being a socially responsible and environmentally conscious company requires a long-term analytical perspective; but shareholders, mutual fund companies, and "Wall Street" analysts still are predominantly focused on the short-term. Similarly, Andre (2012), Resor (2012), Cordle (2012), and Haymore (2011) report on an organization, the non-profit B Lab, which will certify a company as a "beneficial" one if it verifies that it conducts business in an environmentally friendly and socially responsible manner. B Lab does not have regulatory standards *per se*; rather, the organization relies on performance standards to measure and verify CSR (Andre, 2012). "This verification, in turn, helps the company distinguish itself and attract like-minded consumers and investors....Third-party certification may help companies differentiate themselves from a growing barrage of companies claiming to prioritize community and environmental interests. Certification thus improves their ability to attract investment from socially responsible investors ("SRIs") and consumers" (Haymore, 2011, p. 1314). The B Lab ratings system has provisions for:

- Accountability (governance, transparency)
- Employees (compensation and benefits, job creation, employee ownership)
- Work environment
- Consumers (beneficial products and services)
- Community (suppliers, local involvement, diversity, community impact, investor base)
- Charity and service
- Environment (facilities, energy usage, supply chain, manufacturing inputs and outputs)
- Beneficial business models (for employees, consumers, community, and environment) (Andre, 2012).

Resor (2012, p. 102) indicates that B Lab has certified 465 businesses, encompassing 60 industries, and having a combined total of $2.21 billion in revenue. Cordle (2012, p. 5A), writing in 2012, reports that 535 companies worldwide have been certified, which number is up from 370 at the end of 2010, and now representing $3 billion in revenue. Andre (2012) notes, however, that there is a dependence on self-monitoring in B Lab's approach since B Lab allows companies to collect and report their own data without any oversight. Crodle (2012, p. 5A) also notes that there is a social entrepreneurship networking site, called Ashoka, which is a 30 year old non-profit entity based in Washington, D.C., which nurtures social entrepreneurs, totaling today more than 3000 social entrepreneurs in 72 countries.

However, it must be pointed out that the "beneficial" designation by B Lab is not a legal distinction; it is not to be confused with the new legal concept of a "social benefit" or "B-corporation," which will be discussed in a forthcoming section of this work; rather, a B Lab "beneficial" designation is one that any for-profit entity can seek. Of course, B Lab can be used to evaluate any type of corporation. Also, a New York-based organization, the Committee Encouraging Corporate Philanthropy, highlights the social responsibility activities of companies. Companies and projects given the "stamp of approval" by the organization include Wal-Mart's policy to reduce packaging in its supply chain, IBM's Service Corps which sends young executives to help businesses in developing companies, and PepsiCo's program to train corn farmers in Mexico. What is most interesting about the Committee is that it highlights companies and projects that do not "just" benefit the society but that also benefit the companies, such as reducing costs for Wal-Mart, providing business contacts and opportunities for IBM, and increasing the supply of a critical product for PepsiCo. IBM's Corporate Service Core has become very popular since its inception in 2007; and has now fielded more than 200 teams of about a dozen volunteers each, whose assignments include modernizing Kenya's postal service and helping design an online education program in India. The Corporate Service Core program, moreover, has become a "coveted perk" at IBM and one helpful to learning skills and knowledge, developing expertise, as well as helping the career-building of the participants at the company. The goal is to align social responsibility with employee and business objectives. As such, it should be noted that IBM achieved the top position in a social responsibility ranking, called the Civic 50, produced by Bloomberg LP and the National Conference on

Citizenship and Points of Light, which emphasize and measure volunteerism and community benefit from corporate activities. This "selfish" aspect of social responsibility will be discussed further here and by other authors. For now, regarding socially responsible investing, one can clearly see that a great deal of information is available for the socially responsible investor to achieve the laudable goal of doing well by doing "good."

Chapter 8

Corporation "Constituency" Statutes

Socially responsible entrepreneurs and corporate directors and officers who wanted to engage in activities to benefit corporate stakeholders other than shareholders have in the past confronted a serious legal problem. Traditionally, pursuant to state corporation law the directors and officers of a corporation owed legal and fiduciary duties solely to the corporate entity. This overarching duty of the traditional *corpus* of corporate law is described by Resor (2012) as follows:

> The shareholder wealth maximization norm, derived from state corporate law and national corporate norms, stands for the proposition that directors have a duty to maximize shareholder wealth. According to this norm, directors can be held liable for not doing so. If directors of traditional for profit corporations begin to take actions more aligned with those of not-for-profit organizations, the directors might be held liable for violating their fiduciary duties to the shareholders (p. 95).

In fulfilling this duty, the directors and officers, based on the conventional Business Judgment Rule of corporate law, were required to act based on informed consent, with reasonable care, and in good faith. These legal duties were owed strictly and exclusively to the corporation and to the shareholders and not to any other people or groups, though the shareholders might have to enforce these duties on behalf of the corporation, if a breach of these duties by the directors and officers occurred, by means of a shareholder derivative lawsuit.

Today, however, many states have enacted statutes, called "constituency statutes," or have amended their corporation statutes, to allow the directors and officers to consider other constituent groups, often called "stakeholders," who are directly or indirectly affected by the corporation's activities. Millon (2011) states that "as of 2003, forty-one states had enacted 'constituency statutes' that authorize management to take into consideration a range of nonshareholder interests in addition to those of shareholders" (p. 526). Pennsylvania passed the first constituency statute in 1983. The District of Columbia has promulgated such a statute too. Cohen and Schleyer (2012, p. 92) declare that these constituency statutes "…effectively expanded the autonomy and importance of the board of directors…."

Even though some states, such as Delaware, do not have express constituency statutes, nevertheless, the courts have ruled that pursuant to state corporation law the directors of a corporation can consider the effects of corporate actions on non-shareholder groups, such as customers, employees, and perhaps the general community. Millon (2011) notes that "…the Delaware courts have never stated plainly that management fiduciary responsibilities – the duties of care and loyalty – imply a general duty to maximize profits without regard to competing nonshareholder considerations" (p. 527). Millon (2011), furthermore, points out that "in the one situation in which the Delaware Supreme Court has directly addressed management's authority to consider non-shareholder interests, the court has declined to endorse shareholder primacy" (p. 527). Cohen and Schleyer (2012, p. 94) furthermore emphasize that in Delaware there is "…judicial flexibility of board flexibility in determining the appropriate course of action, including, as appropriate, social policy considerations." It also should be mentioned that Delaware is the state of incorporation for almost 2/3rds of publicly traded companies in the United States.

To illustrate express constituency statutes, the Minnesota corporation statute states that "in discharging the duties of the position of director, a director may, in considering the best interests of the corporation, consider the interests of the corporation's employees, customers, suppliers, and creditors, the economy of the state and nations, community and societal considerations, and the long-term as well as short-term interests of the corporation and its shareholders" (*Minnesota Statutes* Section 302A.251(5)). Similarly, in Florida, directors are now permitted to consider in making decisions a variety of factors not directly related to maximizing value for the shareholders. These broader stakeholder factors encompass the long-term interests and prospects of the corporation and its shareholders, as well as the social, economic, legal, or other effects of any corporate action on the employees, suppliers, customers, the communities where the corporation and its subsidiaries operate, and the economy of the state or nation (*Florida Statutes* Section 607.0830(3)). Munch (2012) points out that "there is great variety among the provisions. But most statutes limit the reviewable "stakeholder interests to those of customers, employees, creditors and the local communities" (p. 181). Clark and Babson (2012, p. 830) indicate that "these permissible constituency groups vary state-by-state, but usually include employees, creditors, suppliers, consumers, and the community at large." Consequently, constituency statutes typically are limited, since the definition of "constituents" is a "narrow" one which, although including customers, employees, suppliers, and the local communities where the company does business, does not encompass the international community, environmental concerns, or broader human rights issue. Nevertheless, these statutes, whether separate enactments or amendments to state corporation statutes, usually are called "constituency" statutes.

In the United Kingdom there is similar constituency legislation. Specifically, in the United Kingdom by virtue of the Companies Act of 2006 the directors of British companies are allowed to take into consideration the long-term interests of the corporation, which includes the effect of corporate actions on employees, customers, suppliers, the community, and the environment.

It is critical to note, however, that constituency statutes generally are permissive, and not mandatory; that is, the directors and officers may take into consideration the interests of non-shareholder stakeholders, but the directors and officers are not required to do so. Millon (2011) thus states: "Importantly, however, these statutes only permit balancing of interests rather than requiring it. Corporate boards would thus be free to pursue CSR policies but cannot be sanctioned for choosing not to do so" (p. 526). Similarly, Munch (2012) states that "directors weigh interests at their discretion, and they can freely disregard particular interests without fear of legal consequences at the hands of shareholders or any other group" (p. 181). These constituency statutes do not impose any legal duty on the directors to any newly recognized stakeholders or constituencies, and also that these statutes do not supply a corporate constituency or stakeholder group with a legal cause of action against the corporation's directors. Deskins (2011, p. 1059) points out that "these statutes allow boards of directors to reflect on stakeholder interests in the decision-making process, thus enabling corporations to justify and possibly defend an action that they believe to be in the best interest of the corporation without violating the duties owed to shareholders." Lacovara (2011, pp. 836-38), in examining case law from Pennsylvania interpreting constituency statutes, finds that the courts have declared it "proper" for the directors to consider the effects of a business action, for example, a tender offer to purchase the corporation, on the target company's employees, customers, and communities, and also that the interests of non-shareholder constituency groups could be "synonymous" with the "best interests" of the corporation; but that no case law has suggested that a constituency statute could create a legal duty that would provide an independent cause of action for a non-shareholder stakeholder group. Therefore, regarding non-shareholder interests, these constituency statutes are not mandatory but rather merely "permissive." Resor (2012) describes the problems with constituency statutes, to wit:

> First, constituency statutes do not go beyond what a director can already do in making day-to-day decisions; consider what is in the 'best interest' of the corporation. Second, constituency statutes are often vague and do not contain guidance as to how non-shareholder interests may be considered. Finally, even the most expansive constituency statutes only create the potential for directors to consider the effects of their decisions on non-

shareholder interests, but never allow directors to consider stakeholders interests above shareholders' financial returns (p. 98).

However, two constituency statutes – Idaho and Arizona – require directors to consider the short-term and long-term interests of the corporation in context of stakeholder analysis. "Without granting standing to stakeholders or shareholders, even those states' more stringent constituency statutes are arguably unenforceable" (Munch, 2012, p. 181). Consequently, Clark and Babson (2012, p. 829) conclude that "...even in states that have constituency statutes, the regime of shareholder primacy is still pervasive and the legal framework is not sufficient to meet the needs of new mission-driven and triple-bottom-line businesses."

Chapter 9

Social Benefit Corporations[3]

In marked contrast to the corporate constituency statutes, as well as the traditional corporation itself, is a new legal business concept – the "social benefit corporation." These new entities also are called "benefit corporations," or simply "B-corporations" (as opposed to the traditional business or "C-corporation" of state corporate law). At times, the general term "social enterprise" is used (Resor, 2012, p.92).Very recently in the United States, this new form of business enterprise has been created to provide a corporate legal structure for "social entrepreneurs," that is, those business people who aim to deliver not only financial benefits to the shareholders but also social benefits for local communities and society at large by means of a "double bottom-line" of profits and social benefits or a "triple bottom-line" of social, environmental, and economic concerns. Miller, Grimes, McMullen, and Vogus (2012, p. 616) describe "social entrepreneurship" as follows: "By using market-based methods to solve social problems, social entrepreneurship marries two distinct and ostensibly competing organizational objectives: creating social value and creating economic value." Social entrepreneurs thus form "hybrid organizations that seek to apply market-based solutions to social issues such that benefits accrue primarily to targeted beneficiaries as opposed to owners (Miller, Grimes, McMullen, and Vogus, 2012, p. 618). Andre (2012) states that benefit corporations describe their corporate social responsibility mission broadly "…because their missions suggest potential impacts not only on

---

[3] Coauthored with Bahaudin G. Mujtaba, Nova Southeastern University.

shareholders but on a variety of stakeholders that include customers, employees, communities, and the natural environment" (p. 134).

Udgata and Das (2012, p. 50) define a social entrepreneur as "…a type of entrepreneur who relies on innovation to improve the world through market solutions. Social entrepreneurs use their skills and creativity to try and solve an urgent social problem, with the goal being to make a positive impact. Social entrepreneurs drive social innovation and transformation in various fields, including education, health, environment and enterprise development. They pursue poverty alleviation goals with entrepreneurial zeal, business methods and the courage to innovate and overcome traditional practices. A social entrepreneur, similar to a business entrepreneur, builds strong and sustainable organizations…." Moreover, these "social entrepreneurs believe social good can be produced along with profits, and desire hybrid forms of organization to smooth a single enterprise's path to realizing both goals" (Reiser, 2011, p. 591). Page and Katz (2011, p. 1353) state that "proponents of social enterprise believe that such businesses can combine the dynamism of for-profit firms with the mission-driven zeal more typical of nonprofit enterprises." Lawrence, Phillips, and Tracey (2012, p. 320) combine social entrepreneurship with "social innovation," that is, both "are fundamentally new and innovative ways of organizing, collaborating, and managing that leverage current practices and technologies." Regarding "social entrepreneurs," Munch (2012, pp. 170-71) adds that "while they plan to tackle social problems with business-like ideas and discipline, they also hope for some freedom from the pursuit of profit maximization." Nonetheless, Miller, Grimes, McMullen, and Vogus (2012) state the challenges of being a social entrepreneur:

> Social entrepreneurship is exceptionally challenging, since the entrepreneur not only since the entrepreneur must attempt the founding of an organization but also must work to establish an infrastructure that supports the organization….Often, new markets and new distribution channels must be erected, old cultural stereotypes must be challenged, and innovative revenue streams must be uncovered in the context of minimal disposable

income....In purely economic terms, the personal risks of such an approach are high and the benefits are unknown, rendering the objective plausibility of the associated action are quite low. As such, a rational cost-benefit analysis is unlikely to yield sufficient motivation to create a social enterprise (p. 626).

Similarly, Lawrence, Phillips, and Tracey (2012) state that there are three main challenges to the social entrepreneur "stand out":

First, social entrepreneurs must manage distinctive and complex issues of accountability. While channels of accountability are reasonably clear in private enterprises, with firms accountable to their owners, social entrepreneurs are accountable to multiple consistencies including those that they are seeking to help. Second, social entrepreneurs must manage a "double bottom line." In other words, they must balance social and commercial objectives, which can create tensions within their ventures because social outcomes and commercial performance may need to be traded off against one another. Third, social entrepreneurs need to manage a series of complex identity issues that involve presenting the organization in different ways in order to appear legitimate to actors in both the for-profit and non-profit domains (p. 320).

Indeed, to be a social entrepreneur one must be a very socially responsible, intelligent, motivated, and committed individual who can serve society by using market-based mechanisms.

The concepts of a social business and social entrepreneurs were first conceived by Mohammad Yunus, head of the department of economics at Chitagong University, Bangladesh, the founder of Grameen Bank, and the winner of the 2006 Nobel Peace Prize, for his pioneering work in micro-credit. "Motivated by his belief that credit is a fundamental human right, Yunus's objective was to help people escape poverty by providing loans on suitable terms and education based upon sound financial principles" (Kickul, Terjesen, BacQ, and Griffiths, 2012, p. 453). Yunus believed a social business must be a "viable business enterprise…created and run for the express purpose of pursuing specific, articulated social goals, rather than maximizing profit" (Taylor, p. 1506). Mickels (2009) adds that Yunus wants companies to be "strong" CSR ones, that is, companies which "…seek to benefit people and the planet in the course of doing business so long as the profit margin is not lost" (p. 277). Yunus also wants a strong CSR company to have "…the potential to act as a change agent for the world" (Mickels, 2009, p. 277). Yunus, therefore, was one of the first and most prominent people advocating for a new way of doing business as a corporation – the "social business." Social entrepreneurship, therefore, "…combines a vision and a passion for doing good with a business approach" (Cordle, 2012, p. 5A). One must be cognizant that the terms "social entrepreneurship" and "social business" are typically used synonymously, mainly because they both entail pursuing societal betterment as the goal, there can be a difference because a "social business" can be a business with no dividends. The social entrepreneur now can fit a socially responsible business as well as a social business into the new legal concept in the United States of the social benefit corporation.

The critical difference between a social benefit corporation and a constituency statute is that in a corporation constituency statute the directors of a corporation *may* consider other stakeholder groups than the shareholders, but with a social benefit corporation, the directors *must* consider other stakeholders. In a social benefit corporation, typically in the company's articles of incorporation (which becomes its charter when approved by the state), the corporation will specify its intended social purposes or benefits as well as the stakeholders or constituent groups that it is legally obligated to consider in achieving these objectives. That is, it is pursuant to this new form of doing business the legal duty of corporate directors to consider the consequences of corporate actions, such as moving facilities from one state to another or overseas, lay-offs and downsizing, and takeovers and mergers, on groups other than the shareholders. Moreover, the directors are allowed to consider social responsibility and environmental objectives equal to or even greater than achieving profits. Traditionally, pursuant to state corporation laws, directors were held to a legal duty – a fiduciary duty – to act in the best interests of the corporation and its owners – the shareholders; and consequently directors could not consider stakeholders other than the shareholders. Furthermore, even under constituency states, where directors could consider other non-shareholder stakeholders, the directors had to do so with the aim of maximizing the long-term good, not of the public, but ultimately of the shareholders. For the law in the form of a social benefit corporation to now say that directors have a legal duty, that is, *must*, as opposed to *may*, consider the interests of other stakeholders affected by corporate activities is a very momentous change in the law indeed. It must be emphasized that consideration of the other constituencies beyond the shareholders is "compulsory."

Several states, including Vermont, Hawaii, California, New York, New Jersey, Virginia, North Carolina, Pennsylvania, and Maryland, which in 2010 was the first state, have now promulgated legislation to allow "social benefit" corporations. Legislation has been introduced in Colorado, Michigan, Pennsylvania, North Carolina, and Oregon. The states generally have based their social benefit corporation statutes on a "model" act, called the "Model B-Corp Act" (Lacovara, 2011). So far, the benefit corporation legislation has been done under special statutes, which are separate and distinct from the state's typical business corporation statute. However, Munch (2012) relates that typically "…under these statutes, an existing corporation can elect, upon the approval of two-thirds of the shareholders, to identify and operate as a benefit corporation" (p. 184). Pursuant to the Model Act and the state corporation benefit statutes, typically, the social benefit corporation must be cleared designated as a benefit corporation, and must specify in its social responsibility and environmental objectives in its charter and articles of incorporation, and also in some cases in its bylaws. In Maryland and other states the stock certificates also must be labeled to include the term "benefit corporation." The benefit corporation can pursue a "general public benefit" and/or "specific public benefits," such as providing low income or underserved people or communities with beneficial products or services, promoting economic opportunity for people and communities, preserving, protecting, and improving the environment, improving human health, promoting the arts and sciences, advancing knowledge, and increasing the flow of capital to entities with a public benefit purpose. The Maryland law allows businesses to commit to a specific public good. In Maryland, the specific public benefits can encompass the following: 1) providing individuals and communities with beneficial products and services; 2) providing economic opportunity for individuals or communities beyond the creation of jobs; 3) preserving the environment; 4) improving human health; 5) promoting the arts, sciences, or the advancement of knowledge; 6) increasing the flow of capital to entities with a public benefit purpose; and 7) accomplishing any other particular benefit for society or the environment. However, Reiser (2011, p. 598) emphasizes that "the statutes provide little clarification of the hierarchy of purposes a benefit corporation will serve." Taylor (2011, pp. 1515-16) too is concerned that "to the extent B Corporations articulate general statements about their mission and strive to 'further community interests,' for example, the goals may become more difficult to define. It may then become more challenging to clearly articulate methods of achieving the goals, thus presenting opportunity for intra-corporate disagreement." Page and Katz (2011) assert that the objectives of the social benefit corporation, encompassing profit-maximization, profitability, succession, growth, and liquidity, along with social mission, are all "optimistically claimed" (p. 1368). Three examples of benefit corporations are: 1) Blessed Coffee, a coffee wholesaler, which returns one-half of its profits to its Ethiopian cooperative for use in health clinics, schools, and other local development projects; 2) The Big Bad Woof, a pet food retailer, which contributes significant company resources to animal welfare and rescue efforts; and 3) Patagonia, the out-door clothing company, which is described as an "environmentally conscious" (Munch, 2012, p. 185).

The social benefit corporation statutes require the directors of the corporation to consider the impact of their decision-making not "merely" on the shareholders, but also other corporate stakeholders, such as the employees of the corporation, subsidiaries, suppliers, distributors, customers, the local community, society, and the environment, whether local or global. The social benefit corporation also must publish an annual "benefit report" to disclose the level of performance in attaining those goals as well as any circumstances the corporation's ability to achieve its beneficial purposes. The report must be delivered to shareholders, posted on the company's website, and, in some cases, delivered to the state's Secretary of State (the cabinet level official who typically is in charge of corporate affairs).

Accordingly, regarding non-shareholder, stakeholder groups, "the directors may take action based on the effects of their decisions on any of these groups or interests" (Reiser, 2011, p. 599). For example, in the Maryland statute the directors are required to consider the effects of an action or decision on five difference stakeholder groups: 1) stockholders of the benefit corporation; 2) the employees and workforce of the benefit corporation and the subsidiaries and suppliers of the benefit corporation; 3) the interests of customers; and community and societal considerations. Moreover, Reiser (2011, p. 601) indicates that "all of the statutes anticipate" that independent third parties will assess the performance of the social benefit corporation. Yet Reiser (2011, pp. 601-02) also underscores that "the statutes decline to provide even minimum content for such standards. In addition, they do not dictate how the standards should be applied, how often, and or by whom." So, it must be emphasized that the social benefit corporation statutes neither require a benefit corporation to use any particular third-party standard, to explain why the corporation chose a particular standard, nor to have their benefit report certified or audited by a third party.

The social benefit corporation is thus committed to make a material and positive impact on society as a whole, including the environment (the public or social benefit) as well as to consider the interests of stakeholders or constituency groups other than shareholders. The benefit corporation also must an annual benefit report to the shareholders that includes a description of the ways the company pursued the general or specific public benefits, and the extent to which these benefits were achieved. Cummings (2012, p. 598) refers to this reporting as "social reporting," consisting of 1) an evaluation and verification of the company's socially responsible activities by an independent auditor based on certain benefit standards; 2) the annual public disclosure of the benefit report; and 3) an incentive system for companies who meet their standards, such as a "compliance label," which companies could use on their products as well as in their advertising and marketing. Two benefit standards could be: What percentage of employees participated in company-organized community service days for the last year? And what was the annual percentage of net profits or net revenues that the company gave to charity? Moreover, typically, the social benefit corporation posts its annual report, a self-assessment, and the third party evaluator's report and summary on the B-Corp's website. A benefit corporation typically has a benefits officer who has the responsibility of assessing the company's CSR contributions and activities and who reports them to the third party evaluator. No report, however, usually is required to any government agency.

Page and Katz, 2011, p. 1361) use the term "for-profit social enterprise" for such a benefit corporation, which they define as "...businesses with shareholder-owners that seek to address social problems by combining the dynamism of capitalized for-profit enterprise with the intentionally pro-social orientation of nonprofit organizations." However, this new form of social benefit corporation, it must be pointed out, is neither a tax-exempt entity nor is it non-profit (though a non-profit corporation obviously has a social beneficial purpose). Munch (2012) relates the limitations of a nonprofit organization:

> A nonprofit entity...allows social entrepreneurs extensive freedom to pursue social goals, but it is subject to even greater capital limitations. Nonprofits often must dedicate considerable time, staff, and other resources to fundraising among private donors because they cannot raise funds through private investors. Also, they may have trouble securing favorable loans from banks and other traditional lenders because of their limited and inconsistent access to capital for repayment. And, although abundant government grants are available, these are not necessarily awarded to the most deserving, efficient, or effective nonprofit organizations. Nonprofits

may undertake some commercial activity to support their missions, but their ability to do so is greatly restricted by tax regulations (p. 174).

As such, Lacovara (2011, pp. 842-43) explains that in the United States state "legislators see B-Corp status as a way for a corporation to take on a social mission suited to a nonprofit corporation without taking on a non-profit organization's generally limited liability to attract capital."

Other countries, moreover, have comparable forms of social benefit corporations. For example, the British Community Interest Company (CIC), which has been available in the United Kingdom since 2005, is an alternative way of doing business in order to meet the needs of social entrepreneurs in the United Kingdom. Reiser (2011) points out that, like the U.S. "B-Corp," the CIC is formed for "community benefit" purposes, but it only "...may offer investors limited dividends, but must lock its assets and earnings beyond these limited disbursements into the community benefit stream" (p. 593). Page and Katz (2011) further explain the two key components of the CIC - the "community interest test" and the "asset lock":

> The community interest test is relatively broad. 'A company satisfies the community interest test if a reasonable person might consider that its activities are being carried out for the benefit of the community.' Political campaigning, however, is excluded. The organization also must not limit access to its benefits to too small a group.... 'Asset lock' is the term used for all provisions that endure the CIC's assets and profits are used primarily for the benefit of the community and not for the excessive benefit of employees, contractors, or investors....Investors may buy shares, but dividends are capped, both at a specific rate of return and as a percentage of profits that can be paid in aggregate dividends (pp. 1370-1371).

The CIC also must issue a "community interest company report" together with its annual financial filing; and the CIC is regulated by a government regulator, who can intervene if the CIC no longer meets the community interest test.

Also present in the United Kingdom is the Public Interest Company or PIC. The most important difference between the PIC and the social benefit corporation is that PICs do not obtain equity in private financial markets; rather, PICs are dependent on taxpayer support. Moreover, "in addition to the equity situation, unlike benefit corporations PICs utilize an organizational design that explicitly incorporates stakeholders with the organization....The role of these unpaid stakeholder members is to hold management accountable. Their level of involvement ranges from acting as executive directors to holding infrequent general meetings to discuss operations. These members represent a variety of interested parties including the general public, users, industry experts, and the government" (Page and Katz, 2011, p.146). The stakeholders in a British PIC, therefore, appear to have a much broader and more formal degree of representation that those in the social benefit corporation in the United States.

Of course, a very practical issue emerges regarding such benefit corporations: Why would anyone invest in a company when the economic returns are very likely to be diminished by the benefit objectives when certainly other investment opportunities exist offering the likelihood of greater returns? Taylor (2011) has an answer:

> Several reasons underlie the decision to invest in a social business. On an individual level, an investor's personal identification with and support for the social goals of the business provide strong incentive to become involved. Further, many individuals have a strong impulse to give to 'worthy' causes.... 'Giving' the money to a social business in the form of an investment in a social business is a preferable method of supporting desired goals because the monies invested this way are not simply 'given' but are returned to the investor, who can use that capital again (ideally to invest in another social

business!). Social business investing does not need to replace charitable giving, but can serve as another outlet for those wishing to use their capital to further social good (p. 1507).

Taylor (2011, p. 1506) adds that "stockholders in a social business cannot expect directors to run the enterprise for their benefit because they become shareholders knowing that this is not the case." Munch (2012, p. 188) also states that "any shareholders who approve the use of the benefit corporation, endorse the additional duties and limits it imposes as well." Yet shareholders are not the only group affected.

One problem possibly resulting from the formation of the social benefit corporation is how to find and keep employees who share the company's values and particularly its dual purpose of profit and social responsibility. As Andre (2012) emphasizes, this human resource aspect of the B-Corp "raises several interesting questions." Andre (2012) explains:

> One of these is how in hiring and promotion the benefit corporation might weigh employees' commitment to its CSR mission relative to their technical ability. Another is whether a benefit corporation will attract employees and board members who differ from those attracted to regular corporations. Theoretically, it might attract individuals who are themselves interested in enhancing CSR. Are such workers in benefit corporations more motivated than workers in other corporations? Further, if employees do not see their organizations CSR mission as legitimate, are they more likely to become disaffected than employees who did not care about CSR in the first place? Of course, these are only some of the interesting questions suggested by the benefit corporation design (p. 141).

Another, and very serious, question with the creation of a social benefit corporation is that the law is still developing for this new form of doing business; and consequently the major risk of this new corporate entity is the still un-chartered legal liability of the directors, who not only may be sued by shareholders for not achieving social responsibility goals, but who also may be sued by other stakeholders who are adversely affected by a corporation action which they contend is socially irresponsible to a discrete stakeholder group or injurious to the societal good. This new legal cause of action against directors typically is called a "benefit enforcement proceeding." Resor (2012, p. 109) further explains that "shareholders, directors, parent companies, and any other persons or groups that may be specified in the articles of incorporation can bring an action against a director. The causes of action available to these parties in the benefit enforcement proceedings include a failure to pursue the general public benefit or any specific public benefit set forth in its articles of incorporation." Taylor (2011, p. 1514) succinctly states that "questions…remain about the legal implications of the form." Munch (2012, p. 171) states that the benefit corporation "…raises the most potential legal concerns. Unlike in other types of business associations, where managers are merely permitted to consider stakeholder interests, in the benefit corporation there is a clear affirmative duty to do so." Lacovara (2011, pp. 826-827) emphasizes that the state social benefit statutes provide "little guidance" as to the scope of the expanded legal duties of the directors, particularly whether the social benefit duties are separate and distinct from traditional corporate duties, as well as to what the relationship is between the two sets of duties. Similarly, Taylor (2011, p 1506) maintains that the social benefit business "…requires that traditional corporate fiduciary duty analysis be reconsidered. Shareholder primacy cannot be the driving force behind directorial action." Taylor (2011, p. 1516) sees a paradoxical situation because "…directors of B Corporations would be legally entitled to disregard the notion of shareholder primacy and take other stakeholder interests into account, but they would not be legally entitle to ignore shareholder interests." Moreover, some of the state statutes also decline to address the key issue as to what non-shareholder stakeholder groups have legal standing to sue to enforce the expanded legal duties of the directors. The shareholders of a social benefit corporation now may have expanded rights to bring a derivative suit (pursuant to traditional corporate law against the directors on behalf of the corporation) on behalf of other stakeholders.

Clark and Babson (2012, pp. 849-50) similarly warn of expanded lawsuits from shareholders: "…A shareholder is expressly given the right to bring a legal action on the basis that the director failed to pursue the stated general or specific public benefits, failed to consider the interests of the various stakeholders set forth in the statute, or failed to meet the transparency requirements of the statute….A shareholder could also now bring an action for failure to consider other stakeholder interests (e.g., for failure of the directors to adequately consider the impact of a particular action on the workforce of the company)." Furthermore, the charter of a social benefit corporation can specify other stakeholders who can bring an action against the directors for not achieving public or special benefits. Similarly, Taylor (2011, p. 1515) asks: "…Would the suggested language in a B Corporation's articles of incorporation provide it any real legal protection if it is sued by a shareholder alleging a breach of directorial fiduciary duty for putting stakeholder interests ahead of, even on par with, shareholder interest"? Mickels, 2009, p. 282) is concerned that a benefit corporation may be "creating a risk that directors could be held liable for breaching their fiduciary duty to maximize shareholder profit in favor of benefiting another corporation stakeholder." As such, Mickels (2009, p. 282) asks: "So, must we assume that all publicly held For-Benefit corporations will be subject to shareholder derivative suits for breaching their fiduciary duty"? Lacovara (2011, p. 876) thus criticizes the whole "public benefit concept" as one of "potential vagueness." Chatterji and Richman (2011, p. 34) add that "an inherent and inescapable tension exists between pursuing desirable social outcomes and striving for maximum profits." Lacovara (2011, p. 820), therefore, predicts "inevitable conflicts" as the legal system attempts to define and to reconcile the principles of the legal and fiduciary duty in the context of corporate directors seeking to achieve business objectives and fulfilling social obligations. Similarly, as underscored by the *Wall Street Journal* (Lotten, 2012, p. B1): "That anything other than maximizing shareholder value should be considered in a company's decision-making normally can open the door to investor suits." Lacovara (2011, p. 880) similarly warns of a "hostile legal environment" for social benefit corporations.

Based on the current state of the law and the legal commentary examined for this work, the logical conclusion from the authors' perspective is that the new way of doing business as a social benefit corporation, though well-intended, should be abjured, at least for the present, until the attendant legal rights and responsibilities can be explicated by the courts. Yet social responsibility pursuant to corporate constituency statutes can be a viable legal activity for a company as well as a sustainable and socially beneficial one, of course.

Chapter 10

Low-Profit Limited Liability Companies (L3Cs)

Another very recent innovation in social business entrepreneurship is the low-profit limited liability company, called an L3C, which is a "social" variant of the ordinary limited liability company (LLC). The L3C, though organized as a traditional LLC, is expressly designated as a low-profit entity with explicit charitable or educational objectives. An L3C must pursue a charitable mission, but it also can distribute profits to its investors; yet making profits and the production of income as well as the appreciation of property cannot be the "significant purpose" of the entity (Page and Katz, 2011, p. 1363). Vermont was the first state to enable the creation of L3Cs; and now seven other states, including Montana and Wyoming, also allow these entities. Resor (2012, p. 104) states that, in essence, "L3Cs are designed to accommodate for-profit entrepreneurs with primarily charitable purposes that want to attract program-related investments (PRIs) from foundations." However, the major problem with the L3C, however, is that presently it is not certain that investments in L3Cs will qualify as charitable investments pursuant to federal tax law.

Generally, Resor (2012, p. 92) comments that "the traditional binary organizational system of state corporate law and federal tax law is not suited to accommodate the growing number of organizations with hybrid for-profit and not-for-profit purposes." So, specifically, Taylor (2011, p. 1517) counsels that "...the utility of L3Cs remains in doubt. The efficacy of the L3C designation depends on the willingness of the IRS to support the idea, and there is currently no evidence that it will do so." Furthermore, Page and Katz

(2011, p. 1364) emphasize that "to date, however, the IRS has not granted L3Cs any special privileges by virtue of the designation."

Chapter 11

Social Responsibility and Governance

Corporate governance today has emerged as significant subject for business; and the topic of social responsibility also arises in the context of corporate governance. Initially, one may think of "corporate governance" as having strictly legal components, especially business law and regulatory law. As such, Spector (2012, pp. 42-43) explains: "In the traditional governance models, the corporation's primary focus is on shareholder value rights and the operating decision rule is based on risk to the firm. Directors have a duty to ensure that companies meet their legal obligations, protect shareholder interests, and provide accurate and timely information to investors, regulators, and markets." Corporate governance in a broader sense, however, has several major components: 1) appropriate regulation and governance of the corporation's activities; 2) legislation and agency rules pertaining to the corporation; 3) adhering to the principles of the Utilitarian ethical theory, that is, to do the "greater good for the greatest number"; 4) achieving this greater good without demeaning or disrespecting any stakeholders, as required by the principles of Kantian ethics; and 5) the integration of corporate social responsibility activities into the firm's strategy and policy- and decision-making. As such, corporate governance also has social responsibility as well as ethical ramifications. That is, corporate governance, in the expansive meaning that the author wishes to give to it, means the legal, ethical/moral, and social responsibility considerations for regulating business in the 21st century. Business decision-making cannot be decoupled from the responsibility – legal, ethical, and social - of business leaders for their own risk-taking;

otherwise, the whole business and entrepreneurial system will be "perverted" (Klaus, 2010, p. A19).

The idea is not "just" to maximize profits by "merely" obeying the law, for example, SEC regulations, but rather to also include ethical, moral, and social responsibility concerns into corporate decision-making. Making profits in a legal manner is obviously an essential component to corporate governance, but the focus of "just" the law is too narrow. To illustrate a more expansive meaning of corporate governance, the American Law Institute in its Principles of Corporate Governance sets forth fundamental principles of corporate governance. The primary principle is for the corporation to conduct the business with an objective of enhancing corporate profit and shareholder gain. However, the corporation may take into account ethical considerations that are reasonably regarded as appropriate to the responsible conduct of business; and also the corporation may devote a reasonable amount of resources to charitable, philanthropic, humanitarian, and educational purposes; and the corporation may do so in both situations even if shareholder profit and shareholder gain are not thereby enhanced (American Law Institute, 1994). So, although the primary focus is on the monetary value, this objective is moderated by ethical and social responsibility values, which are then constrained by "appropriate" and "reasonable" qualifications. The idea is that the corporation will engage in self-governance and thus regulate, not only by the strictures of the law, but also by morality and ethics, as well as stakeholder and societal concerns, the manner by which it generates profits. In essence, corporations will act legally, morally, and in a socially responsible manner only if those people who exercise control over the corporation, whether directly or indirectly, that is, the directors, officers, and shareholders together, have the vision to see that the collective future of the business, its stakeholders, and society as a whole is inextricably tied to the sustainability of the entity and the society in which it operates and flourishes, as well as the strength of character and leadership ability to implement and act on that vision.

For the traditional corporation, former Vice-President Al Gore emphasizes a sustainable form of capitalism; and accordingly provides some suggestions on how to structure corporate governance to maximize long-term shareholder, stakeholder, and societal value creation. Specifically, Vice-President Gore wants to empower and motivate business leaders to manage for the long-term by using incentive and compensation systems:

> To begin with, compensation should be aligned with long-term objectives, and financial rewards should be linked to the period over which results are realized. For example, in the asset management industry, we are strong proponents of multiyear rolling performance fees in order to incent investors to manage assets with a long-term perspective....Incentive structures should also reflect more compete measure of performance, for example, increasingly, best practice companies are explicitly including environmental sustainability, customer satisfaction, employee morale and workplace safety in their incentive schemes. These companies understand that these considerations drive long-term financial performance (Gore and Blood, 2010, p. A21).

Mackey and Sisodia (2013) in their book, *Conscious Capitalism*, take a stakeholder approach to the modern business corporation. They contend that the "conscious" business will consider the needs of all its stakeholders, including employees, suppliers, customers, and affected communities, as well as investors. They also believe that a "conscious" business will have "conscious" business leaders, that is, leaders who are motivated not only by the purpose of the business but also by service to its stakeholders. Moreover, based on the practice of the Whole Foods company, they offer suggestions for a corporation governance policy regarding compensation, to wit: a company's pay policies must be transparent so that all the employees know what everyone else is making; the top seven executives make exactly the same in salary and bonuses; and total monetary compensation for the top executives is capped at 19 times the average of the other employees. Business leaders, therefore, must exert – leadership – to improve incentive and compensation systems and other aspects of corporate governance to enhance sustainability.

Corporate governance emerges as a particularly challenging endeavor in the social benefit corporation considering its dual mission of profit-making and societal betterment, the concomitant trade-offs among competing stakeholders, including shareholders, of course, the ensuing competition for corporate resources, the lack of a specific B-Corp government regulator, and the absence in the state legislation as to how the conflicting stakeholder demands should be balanced. As explained by Andre (2012):

> This multiplicity of missions does not confound any relationship with a government regulator because the benefit corporation has no such regulator. The benefit corporation does report to a third party evaluator who examines how well it meets a general CSR mission. On the other hand, internally, that the benefit corporation has multiple missions compounds the complexity of its organizational process for making trade-offs. Managing the needs and interests of multiple different clients – those who want improved human health, an improved environment, and more capital for entities with a public benefit purpose, for example, can only be exceptionally difficult. Indeed, it might be suggested that it is tantamount to running a government (p. 140).

To solve this corporate governance dilemma, the management of the social benefit company can refer to the standards set forth by the third party evaluator to whom the B-Corp must report. Yet since the social benefit corporation legislation provides no concrete guidance, the legislation "…assumes, perhaps, that the top management team will weigh the company's CSR goals in light of their business goals and come to some reasonable decision" (Andre, 2012, p. 140). Andre (2012, p. 142) also suggests "…that to enhance CSR accountability, it may be important that the views of the top management team should be balanced within the company by using participatory designs that do such things as allow for stakeholder representation, invite stakeholder participation, and keep internal communications open." At the very least, due to the mixed mission, vague CSR standards, and conflicting stakeholder demands, the activities of the social benefit corporation should be carefully monitored – by its management, stakeholders, legislators, and citizens.

Chapter 12

CSR and the Advantages of "Going Green"[4]

Corporate social responsibility is recognized as a voluntary and "extra" legal obligations performed by corporations to work for community welfare, "going green," and environmental protection. These socially responsible activities of corporations help them in building a good reputation of "doing well." This reputation of doing well leaves a positive impact on all stakeholders, including the corporation's employees.

Reports and news stories show that many companies and organizations place more concerns on environmental impacts when running their businesses. Due to global climate changes and the realization of the limited natural resources, these organizations are turning their businesses' processes to be eco-friendly. This chapter focuses on the benefits of "going green" and the ways to "go green" in workplaces by emphasizing how organizations can benefit from practicing "going green" in their offices[5]. We have found that there are many organizational and governmental publications that support, encourage, and provide guidelines and valuable information regarding "green" practices for companies. This chapter should be beneficial for managers and business leaders who are looking for ways to "go green" and would like to know about the advantages of "going green" in the workplace.

---

[4] Contributed by Seeting "Grace" Zaelor, Ramkhamhaeng University.
[5] Special thanks go to colleagues in the IB327 course for the their review and contributions in the class project: Emengaha Daniel Ukachukwu, Matthew Dimkpa, Moses Oriabiojie Onaburekhalen, Ogochukwu Michael Osakwe, and Ukakogu Nnaemeka Syluester at the Institute of International Studies, Ramkhamhaeng University

Introduction

Nowadays, one of the most serious global issues is climate and environmental change. A majority of people around the world believe that conserving natural environment is everyone's responsibility. Therefore, many companies take responsibility by promoting "green" practices in their workplaces to help the environment and also to benefit from being socially responsible.

When we are talking about a workplace, it can be an office, a factory, a school, a hospital, or any place that the work, products, or services are performed and produced. There are many different ways to change the workplace to be more eco-friendly to protect the environment, for example, ways to save electricity, water, paper, as well as recycling waste. By changing the practices in a workplace, the company not only saves natural resources but also reduces costs that they have to pay both directly and indirectly. Some practices can help the company to consume less time and efforts in certain kinds of situations. These sustainability promotions can also improve a company's public image, which will result in increased business opportunities for a long-term. Many large companies are shifting to "green" businesses and then acknowledging the benefits they gain from such socially responsible efforts, as well as asking for regulations to control greenhouse gas emissions (Linn, 2007).

There are organizational and governmental entities that support companies to take actions on changing the working environment to be more eco-friendly with guidelines and advisements. As the idea of "going green" keeps expanding, companies are not only encouraging their employees to "go green," they also encourage their stakeholders like suppliers, stockholders, and people in the community to practice "green." As a result, more consumers will prefer to buy products and services from "green" companies because they are aware of necessity to "go green" and protect the environment.

Ways to "Go Green" in a Workplace

Most of us may have been taught how to "go green" when we were in school, for example, turning off lights and water faucets when not in use, dispose waste in designated areas to reduce land pollution, and planting trees around the school to improve the environment. Sustainability practices in a workplace are almost as simple as that. Some of the ways to "go green" are to reduce electricity, water, and paper usage, recycle as many things as possible, think about sustainability when making business decision, and encourage employees and people in the community to get involved in sustainability business plan.

We can reduce electricity, water, and paper usage by turning off and unplug electronic equipment when not in use or fully charged, minimizing the use of computer and printer by reusing and refilling a printer cartridge, printing on both sides of paper in black instead of in color, using recycled paper or organic paper, keeping documents and files on computers rather than printing them out, recycling paper, glass, and plastic products.

Encouraging people to practice "green" may take some efforts. We have to start with our employees by enforcing some policies and providing guidelines, for example, we have to restrict smoking area and never smoke in the office to maintain healthy air flow, use bicycle or walking to travel between home and office when possible, and combine trips to save energy and reduce air pollution. If we bring lunch to the workplace, make sure to use insulate lunch bag, and try to make organic meals, as it is not only good for the environment, but also good for our health.

Once we know how to "go green" in a workplace, we should be confident of "going green." We don't have to be managers to start "going green," we can start from ourselves. Encouraging and educating people around you to practice "green" can make a big difference when they learn the importance of sustainability.

Advantages of "Going Green" in a Workplace

Reduce costs for company. When companies set "going green" policies, they are reducing their costs. The costs that can be reduced are utility bills, some office equipment costs, health insurance costs, as well as gaining some tax exemption. There are also other minor costs that can be reduced through "going green" process, such as buying "green" products that are eco-friendly and have longer lifetime than regular products.

Reducing the electricity bill can be done by turning off the lights and other electronic utilities after using. We may have heard that it consumes more power to turn the light on than to keep it on, but this is not true because they actually consume the same amount of energy. Moreover, if the workplace is well designed that sunlight is sufficient for certain kinds of workplace, there is no need to turn the light on during day time. Another way is to use energy-saving light bulbs at the workplace instead of regular light bulbs. Although some energy-saving bulbs may have a slightly higher price, such a bulb has a longer lifetime and can save energy in a long term.

Preservation of water saves a lot of money in a company. This can be done by using a shower reduction set that will help to reduce the amount of water usage when the faucet is turned on, taking fast shower, turning off water faucets when finish using, and repairing the leaky areas.

Some office utilities costs can be reduced by buying recycled paper and "green" office equipment that can be reused and thus not be harmful to the environment. The more paper a company buys, the more storage and storing process the company has to take care of. Once a company has a "green" workplace, it is healthy for their employees to work there and will result in reduction of health issues and costs. There are sustainability practices that reduce costs directly and indirectly as some countries enforce tax reduction regulation on companies that can reduce carbon dioxide emission. For example, according to *Climate Change Agreements Scheme* of the United Kingdom government, a company in the United Kingdom that successfully reduces carbon dioxide in business process will qualify for Climate Change Levy which provides discount rate for 90% of electricity and 65% of other fuels.

Reduce Process and Time. Information technologies have been developing rapidly recently. Such technology provides us the opportunities to process with less paper in our workplace, communicate a message by e-mail instead of making a hard copies, and store data in the computer instead of using paperwork. This benefit not only helps the environment, it also helps us to save a lot of time and process in a workplace.

When we use available information technology in a workplace, we can send e-mail to our co-workers or teams in less than five minutes without using paper. Although it is advised that employees should not use e-mail for important messages, it is recommended to use e-mail when sending short or regular notification messages.

There are many services that are provided through the Internet instead of filing or mailing paperwork. Many companies have ideas of "going green" between the processes of service providing in which the customers can choose to receive "green" services through phone and Internet, for example, credit card monthly statement, and utility bills that will be e-mailed to customers' email addresses in electronic file format to save time and processes.

One of the leading technologies in business world is Virtual Private Network, which provides spaces for businesses to host their data and develop their webpage so that customers and employees can access to data stored on the server without having to waste their time to visit the actual location. This Internet network accessing led to teleworking that not only saves time and processes, but also gives employees opportunities to manage their time and work processes.

Although "going green" in a workplace by providing services through phone and Internet can save time and process, we still have to deal with security and privacy concern by setting password protection and authentication when accessing data server. Once we know how to deal with this concern, this sustainability option can be extremely useful.

Reduce Impact on Environment. Environmental impacts from workplaces can be in many different forms. The impacts can be air pollution, land pollution, water pollution, or noise pollution. Pollutions are basically any changes made to natural resources and cause the resources to be unusable or harmful to be used.

By "going green" in a workplace, these impacts on environment can be reduced in many ways. For example, reducing the use of paper can reduce paper waste, which will cause land pollution and reduce trees that are being cut down to make paper, using organic or healthy raw materials in the type of a workplace like factory can reduce water, land, and air pollution by releasing waste that does not affect environment, and manage any harmful waste properly. Noise pollution can be reduced by using material that will minimize the noise when constructing the factory and use proper tools for factory works. In this way, we are not only preventing pollution but we can also conserve natural resources by using energy in an effective way. As natural resources are running out, we can learn to buy "green" products to use in our workplaces. One good daily practice is to put food waste to its good use by recycling unsalable materials which will help to reduce waste disposal for a workplace, cafeteria, or food suppliers.

We can see that sustainability in a workplace can help us to save costs and protect the limited natural resources. A report on *Fortune 500 Partners List* shows that some of the top energy and software companies like Intel, Microsoft, Apple, and Cisco are sourcing their energy from solar, wind, biogas, small-hydro, and biomass to minimize consumption of energy from coal and fuels. The use of sunlight and wind is one of the unlimited natural resources that more and more companies and other entities are placing interests in as a great way for sustainability.

Improve Public Image and Business Opportunities

A "green" company that buys "green," thinks "green," acts "green", and sells "green" has selling points that can give the company a good public image and lead to good public relations. Although there are many great advertisement strategies, having a good public image from the fact that the company is a "green" organization that actually cares about the environment can have a great impact on sales and future promotions.

According to *Green Business* article, researchers found that larger companies tend to have sustainability plans for their businesses in their agenda more than small and private companies because of consumers' pressure that demand "green" goods, based on several researches and surveys (Swallow & Furniss, 2011). If a company strongly promotes sustainable practices, the policies, process, and results are usually included in the company's report. This will help to promote the company and allow people and organizations in the community to have good concepts about the company because they like it when companies "go green." Then they can spread the words about that company's good image that they have values of caring and protecting the environment by "going green" in the workplace. These values will lead your organization to step higher.

When a company has established a good public image with "going green" programs in the workplace, one lifelong benefit that they gain is increment in business opportunities. Such business opportunities include customers and companies who prefer to buy products and services from companies with green standards, organizations that set "green" standards as one of the requirements of signing a contract, attract competitors' customers with positive public relation, and to be recognized in a positive fashion by other organizations in the community which will lead to a good network in the future.

According to *Greening Your Products: Good for the environment, good for your bottom line,* 2002, the number of companies that emphasize environmental conservation has been increasing these years. Many companies are using "green standards" set by EPA (Environmental Protection Agency) as the standards to determine whether a company is "green" or not. Some organizations are only willing to negotiate to sign contracts with "green" companies. As the idea of "going green" in the business world expands, consumers also set the level of "green" business apart from regular business. Although "going green" may not be the selling point for every type of business, it can be the winning point when consumers make comparison with business' competitors. EPA also holds a program called EPP (Environmentally Preferable Purchasing) that functions like a shopping mall for consumers who prefer to "shop green" and employees who would like to work in a "green" company. EPP has a list of businesses with qualified "green" standards that is available to public.

There are many agencies in addition to the EPA that are encouraging companies to "go green" by giving them advisement, guidelines, and profit to go green. If a company has a "green" workplace, they have an opportunity to participate in a network that gathers companies with green practices. It is a lifelong benefit to be in such a network, be recognized by people in the community, and to draw favorable attention to consumers by promoting "green" practices, because more and more people are aware of the importance of protecting nature.

Summary

As information technology keeps developing and natural resources keep decreasing, one of the ways to use technology effectively to help protect the environment is to "go green" in a workplace. There are many advantages a company can gain by "going green" and these advantages will last for a long time.

The advantages of "going green" in a workplace include, reduction of a company's costs, reduction of working process and time, reduction of impacts on environment, improvement of a company's public image, and increment on business opportunities. There are also other advantages that are not included in this paper, and thus which should be subjects for further research. For example, "green" practices in a workplace can lead to further development of working policies and technology that emphasize protecting the environment.

Some of the challenges that companies promoting sustainability may face are the change in processes, cost, and value of the companies that they have to solve "green" challenges with innovative ways. In order to properly benefit corporate performance, sustainability must be paired with innovation. Without innovation, simply committing to improve the organization's sustainability performance is likely to detract from financial performance (Chandler, 2012).

We can see that more and more governmental and non-profit organizations are promoting and encouraging business to "go green." This awareness and pressure will lead more people to place serious emphasis on conserving the environment. This emphasis on social responsibility and preserving the environment means more consumers will likely buy "green" products and services, more suppliers will like to sell "green" materials, and more people in the community will want to support "green" business. Therefore, it definitely is time to start "going green" in a workplace. The "win-win" result will be the protection and preservation of the environment, an enhanced and deserved reputation for social responsibility and sustainability, and accordingly very tangible benefits accruing to the organization and its stakeholders, including society as a whole. "Going green," therefore, is the right thing to do as well as the smart thing to do!

Chapter 13

CSR and Human Resource Management in a Spiritual Context[6]

Corporate social responsibility implies that human resource professionals should provide flexibility in the organization so managers can take care of their employees' spiritual needs. Human resource management (HRM) today is at the center stage for enhancing organizational competitiveness and employee self-fulfillment. The general approach (among both academicians and practicing managers) toward effective HRM is primarily based on material considerations with the result of a perpetual tug-of-war between principals and agents at various levels of organization. This chapter attempts to "plug-the-gap" in knowledge by looking at HRM from a holistic perspective of Islam as a means of achieving cooperative excellence (win-win approach) in the work-setting. The emphasis of such an attempt would be to "dig out" Islamic foundations of HRM and then to propose an HR model based on a spiritual contract for contemporary organizations.

Introduction

A major challenge for organizations today and in the future seems likely to be an ever more urgent search for competitive advantage. This challenge is the result of the emergence of knowledge economy, demographic changes, and the technological revolution, which have brought about both threats and opportunities. It is increasingly argued that the organizations best able to meet this challenge will be those

---

[6] Contributed by Muhammad Zeb Khan, FAST-National University, Peshawar, Pakistan.

that can acquire and utilize valuable, scarce, and inimitable resources (Barney, 1995). Human resources can fall into this category, particularly if they are effectively deployed through appropriate human practices and the management of organizational culture (Barney and Wright, 1998). The contribution of Human Resources to the success of an organization has been emphasized through the doctrine of "excellence quality, innovation, and entrepreneurship." These developments have placed the management of people firmly on the priority attention; and also have created the conditions for the emergence of a new-style theory of personnel management. The need of HRM is felt much more now than ever before. The traditional sources of success—product and process technology, protected or regulated markets, access to financial resources, and economies of scale—can still provide quality, technology, and the economies of scale—can still provide competitive leverage, but to lesser degree now than in the past (Pfeffer, 1995), primarily because they have become easier to imitate (Becker and Huselid, 1998) and hence are not sustainable. The implications of this shift are: First, managers must focus on "identifying and solving the human capital elements of important business problems that are likely to impede growth, lower profitability, and diminish shareholder value; Second, top management must treat the HR system as a potential strategic lever for the organization (Becker *et al.*, 1997).

The organization-employee relationship in modern world is primarily said to be governed by a formal contract and a psychological contract. Formal contract explicitly documents the rights and obligations of both parties and its breach may have legal consequences whereas the psychological contract is a kind of tacit understanding of expectations of both parties and its breach may have profound implications other than legal ones. In a society governed by Islamic principles, the employee-organization interaction is influenced by a spiritual contract. This contract is part of an overarching Muslims' belief system that demands complete submission to the will of Allah in every sphere of life.

This chapter attempts to explore the Islamic underpinnings of Human Resource Management (HRM) and relate them to modern thinking, which is based predominantly on materialistic considerations. By doing so, the study in question will come up with a model of HRM that govern organization-employee interaction in an environment which is partly or completely influenced by the Islamic perspective of life. This study would enhance one's understanding of the role and effectiveness of HR policies and practices informed by formal and psychological contract vis-à-vis the spiritual contract inspired by Islam. Based on the HRM principles expounded in the holy Quran and Sunnah, the chapter concludes that the relationship between employees and organizations could be mutually rewarding if both the parties subordinate their formal and psychological contracts to the spiritual contract of Islam.

Problem Statement

Employees and the organizations need each other. Employees want organizations to provide them an enabling environment, rewarding and secure jobs, growth opportunities, and fair treatment. In short, they want self-fulfillment. An organization, on the other hand, wants its employees to perform their duties diligently and honestly, cooperate with others, and stay committed to the organization's goals.

In order to ensure that both parties achieve their respective goals without letting one party exploit the other, the relationship is founded and governed by formal contracts which specify, as much as possible, their rights and obligations. In practice, the parties may or may not live up to their obligations due to many factors including the poor definition of contracts, organizational change, and the human nature that ultimately lead to conflicts manifested in different ways. Historically, there have been various attempts by researchers and practicing managers to find ways for goal-alignment (convergence of interests). The latest approach is human resource management but the results have been less than what to be desired given the fact that both parties depend primarily on external controls and material considerations. An important element missing from the equation is accountability to the transcendental Reality, which Muslims call Allah.

This chapter attempts to fill the gap in human knowledge by incorporating the spiritual contract in the field of human resource management (HRM). It is argued in this chapter that organizations best able to strengthen this spiritual contract will be more productive, responsible, and peaceful than others that depend on formal and psychological contracts alone.

Literature Review

The prevalent human resource policies and practices shape the day-to-day behavior of employees and signal to employees the terms of their employment (Hiltrop, 1995). For example, selection, training, and reward systems send cues to employees on what the employer is willing to offer as part of the relationship and at the same time signal to employees what their contributions are to the relationship. According to Armstrong (2009), employees may expect to be treated fairly as human beings, to be provided with work that uses their abilities, to be rewarded equitably in accordance with their contribution, to be able to display competence, to have opportunities for further growth, to know what is expected of them and to be given feedback on how they are doing. Employers may expect employees to do their best on behalf of the organization, to be fully committed to its values, to compliant and loyal, and to enhance the image of the organization with its customers and suppliers. Thus, in employment relationship, an employee has to seek answer to two fundamental questions: 'what can I reasonably expect from the organization?' and 'what should I reasonably be expected to contribute in return?' Guest et al (1996) contend that the psychological contract may provide some answer to the above questions.

Schein (1980) maintained that psychological contract is a key determinant of employees' attitudes and behaviors in the workplace. Rousseau (1995) suggested that employees derive the terms of their psychological contract in three main ways. First, individuals may receive persuasive communications from others. When being recruited, prospective employees may receive implicit or explicit promises from recruiters or interviewers. Once hired, coworkers and supervisors may describe their view of the obligations that exist between employees and the employer. Second, employees' observations about how their coworkers and supervisors behave and are treated by the organization act as social cues that inform employees of their contractual obligations. Third, the organization provides structural signals such as formal compensation systems and benefits, performance reviews, and organizational literature, including handbooks and missions statements that all play a role in the creation of the employees' psychological contract.

The power relations may change over time leading to the breach of psychological contract. The contract breach has been defined as an employee's belief that the organization has failed to fulfill its obligations to the employee (Morrison & Robinson, 1997) or vice versa. The breach of contract (perceived or actual) by either party and for any reason may translate into different consequences including employee frustration and trust deficit (Robinson, 1996), low commitment to the organization (O'Leary, Kelly et al, 1999), job quits and poor job performance (Millard, 1998). Research on the psychological contract has focused on antecedents, outcomes and processes of contract breach. When fulfilled, the psychological contract would be expected to have positive effects on employee performance. This is because the reciprocity norm would encourage employees to fulfill their contractual obligations to the organization (Coyle-Shapiro and Kessler, 2002). Despite this, according to (Morrison and Robinson, 1997) contractual breach may occur due to *incongruence* (misunderstanding with the organization*), disruption* (circumstances beyond an organization's control*), or reneging* (willful act by the organization*)*. The breach of contract (formal and psychological) may be eliminated or minimized in an environment where employees and managers (or employers) believe in accountability to a transcendental Reality. For Muslims, it means the strength of their faith (spiritual contract) determines their attitudes and behavior in work setting. Islam demands total submission to the Will of Allah: "O ye who believe! Come, all of you, into submission (unto Him); and follow not the footsteps of the devil. Lo! He is an open enemy for you (Al Quran: Chapter 2, Verse, 208)". The conditions for everlasting success or *falah* in Islam are the same for all Muslims whether carrying out their organizational duties and responsibilities or conducting their daily activities. For seeking inspiration and guidance in all their affairs, Muslims are directed to resort to the holy Quran and Sunnah. Allah says, "And obey Allah and the Messenger, that ye may find mercy (Al Quran: Verse, 132, Chapter 3). In addition to this, Muslims are supposed to fulfill their obligations toward Allah and His creatures. "Keep the covenant. Lo! of the covenant it will be asked" (Al-Quran: Verse 34, Chapter 17). Thus, any contract a Muslim enters into with someone (an individual or organization) has got religious sanctity in addition to legal backing. The breach of contract by a Muslims is considered to be a sign of hypocrisy and weak faith. The Prophet said, "The signs of a hypocrite are three: one, whenever he speaks, he tells a lie; two, whenever he promises, he always breaks (his promise); third, if you trust him, he proves to be dishonest (Bukhari, Vol. 1, Book 2, No. 32).

In the search of pleasing Allah, Muslims have to honor their covenants and fulfill their obligations as ordained in the holy Quran and the Sunnah of His last Messenger. Employment, therefore, constitutes a noble activity governed by Islamic injunctions (Spiritual Contract) that ensures an organization's success and individual self-fulfillment.

Spiritual Contract

Islam is more than just a belief - it is a complete way of life, because it goes beyond acts of worship to embrace all one's social and economic activities, thus the Islamic work ethic goes well beyond that of the Protestant work ethic (Ali, 2008). Spiritual contract in the context of Islam may be defined as a covenant between Allah and a Muslim in which the latter submits to Allah in return for getting Falah (enduring success) in this world as well as in the hereafter. According to the Holy Quran: "Lo! Allah hath bought from the believers their lives and their wealth because the Garden will be theirs: they shall fight in the way of Allah and shall slay and be slain. It is a promise which is binding on Him in the Torah and the Gospel and the Qur'an. Who fulfilleth His covenant better than Allah? Rejoice then in your bargain that ye have made, for that is the supreme triumph" (Al-Quran: Verse No. 111, Chapter 9). Islam is not confined to performing a few rituals but offers a comprehensive code of conduct. For Muslims, as employees and employers, Islam provides broad principles for mutual interaction with special emphasis on halal (permissible in Islam) earning. The holy Quran enjoins, "O' mankind! Eat of that which is lawful and wholesome in the earth, and follow not in the footsteps of the devil. Lo! He is an open enemy for you (Al-Quran: Verse 168, Chapter 2). The conditions for everlasting success or *falah* in Islam are the same for all Muslims – whether carrying out their organizational duties and responsibilities or conducting their daily activities. A Muslim, thus, enters into a spiritual contract with Allah that governs his or her entire life.

Any agreement a Muslim enters into is subordinate to his covenant with Allah which is reflected in "La Ilaha illallah, Muhammad-ur-Rasullulah," meaning that there is no god but Allah and Muhammad is His messenger. This declaration and conviction binds a Muslim to submit to Allah and obey His messenger in all activities of life including employment. The Holy Quran says, "O ye who believe! Obey Allah, and obey the messenger and those of you who are in authority; and if ye have a dispute concerning any matter, refer it to Allah and the messenger if ye are (in truth) believers in Allah and the Last Day. That is better and more seemly in the end (Al-Quran: Chapter No. 4, Verse No. 59) and "obey not the command of the transgressor (Al-Quran: Chapter No. 26, Verse No. 151). If, however, the agreement a Muslim enters with anyone (individual or organization) is in line with Islamic injunctions, he or she has to carry it out in letter and spirit.

Islamic Model of HRM

The spiritual contract lies at the heart of HRM model. Divine inspiration strengthens the relationship between employee and employer. Both parties believe that unfulfilled commitments and/or exploitation of the other party would cause the wrath of Allah (SWT); whereas fulfillment of mutual obligations would fetch huge rewards in the form of productive and cordial relationship in this world in addition to attaining eternal salvation in the life hereafter. Contrary to the traditional model of HRM which emphasizes material considerations in employee-employer relationship, the Islamic model of HRM accords more importance to its spiritual aspect. The underlying assumption is that the Muslims derive more satisfaction from their actions carried out in pursuit of getting the pleasure of Allah (SWT). This, however, does not mean that material rewards are meaningless. The point is that spirituality takes precedence over material rewards. Figure 13.1 shows a spiritual model of human resources management.

Figure 13.1 - Model of HRM based on Spiritual Contract

This model shows the nature of employee-organization relationship based on spiritual contract. The main emphasis of the model is on the submission of both employees and employers (organizations) to Allah (SWT). It is argued that both parties should seek inspiration as well as guidance from their original contract with Allah (SWT). Even if one party deserts on either of the two contracts (Formal and Psychological), even then the other party has to preserve the sanctity of the spiritual contract. In essence, it means "two wrongs do not make a right."

Understanding the HRM based on Islamic principles has important implication for contemporary organizations operating in a Muslim country, or employing people with Islamic beliefs, or contemplating social responsibility activities. The genesis of this spiritual contract is the belief that every Muslim has dual accountability: One, accountability of employees expressed in terms of loyalty, performance, and honesty to the organization they work in and two, their inner feeling of answerability for their actions on the Day of Judgment. Conversely, the employers too have dual responsibility in dealing with employees: one, they have to ensure that the HR policies and practices fulfill requirements of their faith and two, they are in line with overarching business strategy.

Employee Self-fulfillment and Organizational Performance

Employees join organizations with an expectation that their physiological, psychological, and social needs would be fulfilled in return for their contribution. Similarly, an organization expects its employees to work efficiently and responsibly to ensure that the organization achieves its tactical and strategic goals. In other words, both employees and organizations strive for self-fulfillment and performance.

Self-fulfillment is an ideal which consists in carrying to fruition one's aspirations and potentialities. It represents a life which is well lived, deeply satisfying, and meaningful. It is an intrinsic value desired for itself and is marked by choice, creativity, and capacity development (Rogers, 1961). Like a seed which grows into a tree naturally under favorable conditions, the employees (if given a chance) tends to develop their potentialities into perfect human (Horney, 1951). In pursuit of self-fulfillment, employees may demand flexible time, involvement in decision-making, interesting and rewarding jobs, and an enabling environment (Pfeffer, 1994). On the other hand, organizations want their employees to be loyal, work efficiently, and demonstrate honesty. Apparently, there is conflict of interest between the two parties. In order to resolve the inherent divergence of interests, organizations and employees mostly depend on formal mechanisms (formal contracts, policies, monitoring mechanisms, appraisal systems, etc.) or cultural controls (beliefs, norms, values, etc.). Both structural and cultural controls are subject to manipulation by the powerful party (mostly the organization) and use them as tools of exploitation (Marx, 1867).

How can the spiritual contract ensure the convergence of interests (win-win situation) between employees and organization? In terms of self-fulfillment, and organizational performance, spiritual contract offers a better and viable solution. Incorporating Islamic principles, which Muslims believe are based on justice, in the equation of employee-organization relationship would minimize (if not completely eliminate) the chances of conflicts. The spiritual contract acts as a neutral arbiter between the two parties. In other words, in the event of any conflict or disagreement, the matter in question can be referred to Allah (the principles laid down in the holy Quran) for resolution.

The Quran says, "Believers! Obey God, His Messenger, and your (qualified) leaders. If you have faith in God and the Day of Judgment, refer to God and His Messenger concerning matters in which you differ. This would be a more virtuous and a better way of settling differences (Verse 59, Chapter 4)". The Muslims are supposed to submit to the will of Allah without any ill will in their hearts. In the words of the holy Quran, "I swear by your lord that they will not be considered believers until they let you judge their disputes and then they will find nothing in their souls to prevent them from accepting your judgment, thus, submitting themselves to the will of God (verse 65, chapter 4). The principles laid down in Islam protect the interests of both parties (employer and employee) of the contract. For ensuring convergence of interests of an organization and its employees and governing their relations smoothly, the following broad principles have been laid down in Islam and constitute the basis of spiritual contract.

Intention (Nya): In Islam, every act should precede by intentions. The Prophet Muhammad is reported to have said, *"The reward of deeds depend upon the intentions (Sahih Bukhari, Hadith 01, The Book of Revelation).* The ultimate purpose of a Muslim's action is to please Allah (SWT) who is Omnipresent and Omnipotent. This implies that policies, procedures, and rules are essentially meant for guidance and coordination rather than a means of effective accountability. A true believer does not need external structures for control more than he/she depends on internal self-control (faith).

Consultation (Shura): The second important management principle in Islam is consultation. In normal circumstances, the manager/leader has to consult subordinates/followers in all issues before taking an action. Involving people in decision making has many advantages including employee development and sense of ownership. The Quran says, "Forgive *them and ask God to forgive (their sins) and consult with them in certain matters* (chapter 3, verse

159)". Moreover, the Muslims have been commended in the Quran for conducting their affairs with consultation (chapter 14, verse 38).

Trust (Amana): The principle of trust is a core value governing social, economic, and political relationships of Muslims. Every person is held accountable for his/her doings in the community. The Holy *Quran* states: *'O you that believe! Betray not the trust of God and the Apostle nor misappropriate knowingly things entrusted to you'* (Chapter 8, verse 27). In the organization context, both the employer and employee have to take proper care of the authority and duties entrusted to them. A true believer has to guard against any temptations of corruption (the abuse and/or misuse of authority). The Quran enjoins, "God *commands you to return that which had been entrusted to you to the rightful owners. Be just when passing judgment among people. God's advice is the most noble, He sees and hears everything (Chapter 4, verse 58)"*.

Bearing Witness (Shahada): The principle of Shahada is somewhat related to whistle-blowing in modern management. This principle states that one has to transcend personal interest and raise voice for justice. A Muslim is not supposed to be a passive recipient of tyranny in any form and manifestation. God says in the holy Quran, *"Believers, be steadfast for the cause of God and just in bearing witness. Let not a group's hostility to you cause you to deviate from justice (Chapter 5, verse 8).* However, in trying to prevent any injustice and oppression, one has to use legitimate means and never resort to any tactics, which cause more harm than doing any good. In other words, both the "ends" as well as the "means" to attain them must be justified. The holy Quran enjoins, *"Call to the path of your Lord through wisdom and good advice and argue with them in the best manner (chapter 16, verse 125)"*.

Halal (Pure) Earning: Over and above fulfilling legal requirements in earning, a Muslim is supposed to ensure that he or she is complying with Islamic injunctions in earning. Halal rizq (pure provision) in essence is a form of worship duly rewarded in the Hereafter. The holy Quran says, "Eat from the pure and lawful things that God has given to you. Have fear of God in Whom you believe (Chapter 5, verse 88)". The concept of halal earning has implication for employees as well as employers. A true believer, as per this principle, would avoid earning by means of fraud, embezzlement, and other forms of corruption.

Justice (Adl): Exploitation in all its forms and manifestation is prohibited in Islam. People in authority have no right to administer selective justice and make decisions that reflect favoritism and/or nepotism or other ulterior motives. All actions of a Muslim must have legitimacy which flows from the holy Quran and the Sunnah (sayings and deeds of the Prophet Muhammad peace be upon him). The Quran says, "Believers, be steadfast for the cause of God and just in bearing witness. Let not a group's hostility to you causes you to deviate from justice" (verse 8, chapter 5). In the context of HRM, it implies that a Muslim in his capacity as employer or employee has to act according to the notion of justice. Justice, both distributive as well as procedural, should manifest itself in all HR functions including hiring, promotion, appraisal, compensation, and discipline. Similarly, a Muslim employee has to carry out his/her duties regardless of the monitoring system in place.

The spiritual contract between employer and employee is grounded in the principles laid down above. The stronger this contract, the greater are the chances of achieving win-win sustainable relationships between organizations and their employees.

Summary

Muslim writers argue that it is necessary to imagine an alternative economic order which is determined by particular Islamic principles to perform a socially responsible as well as integrative function: that of incorporating Islamic values and ethics into the practices of everyday life, including economic transactions (Taqiuddin, 2002). The chief characteristic of the Islamic Concept of Life, according to Mawdudi (1996) is that it does not admit a conflict, nay, not even a significant separation between life–spiritual and life–mundane. It does not confine itself merely in purifying the spiritual and the moral life of a person in the limited sense of the word. Its domain extends to the entire gamut of life.

In every age, some form of morality conducive to social harmony has been preached, but explaining the rationale underlying this morality has always been fraught with difficulties. Morality seems to set out a code for ideal relations between human beings (Rodinson, 1973). After the Industrial Revolution, most people work for organizations to earn their livelihood and hence interact with entities that have their own legal personality. To have a productive and meaningful relationship between employees and the organizations they work in, it is necessary to have mutual trust which can be developed and sustained if both parties submit to certain moral principles. Islam as a complete way of life provides a moral framework within which both employees and organizations have to perform their duties. This moral compass which guides employee-organization interaction is what the spiritual contract is all about.

The efficacy of the spiritual contract requires faith in Allah and the life hereafter. This contract, therefore, leads to employees' self-fulfillment and better organizational performance in organizations operating in an Islamic environment. Generalizing it to other environments is limited to how employees or the organization make sense of life. The capitalist economic paradigm reduces life to material satisfaction which means a transactional relationship between organizations and their employees. The natural corollary of such a relationship is a constant tug-of-war with possibilities of exploitation of either party. The spiritual contract, on the other hand, emphasizes the need to let employees work as part of their spiritual development and let the organizations provide an enabling environment characterized by justice, employee involvement, human dignity, and social responsibility. Many verses of the *Quran* speak about justice and honesty in trade, courtesy and fairness in employment relationships, and also encourage humans to learn new skills and to strive to do good work, which benefit both the individual and the community. Islam emphasizes co-operation in work and consultation in making decisions (Abuznaid, 2006).

Chapter 14

Implications and Recommendations

The new corporation structure of the social benefit corporation is clearly a problematic one for business people, directors, and entrepreneurs, even very socially responsible ones. The law is just too new and unsettled as to nature of the public benefit and especially as to the legal risks of being a director of a "B-corp." As such, no corporate board of directors wants to be the "test case" in determining the parameters of legal liability under a social benefit corporation model. Similarly, with the very new L3C way of doing business socially until the IRS promulgates some precise rules, this entity, again though laudatory, is to be avoided. Nonetheless, socially responsible people who plan to incorporate can always include social responsibility goals in the articles and bylaws of a traditional corporation, and the typical state's constituency statute expressly allows the consideration of other stakeholder groups. So, the legal latitude exists to be socially responsible, yet without mandating a legal duty on the board to be socially responsible. Moreover, the authors have argued that it is in the long-term, egoistic, self-interest of the corporation to be a socially responsible one, and thus to be active and engaged in community, civic, and charitable activities.

Yet what exactly is the effect of all these social responsibility efforts on the "bottom-line"? This critical fact is difficult to ascertain due to the need for more research as well as the need for a longer-term perspective. This book has presented one such study. Another academic study, conducted by Schnietz and Epstein (2005), found that there is value to a corporation during a crisis by having a reputation for corporation social responsibility, and, in particular that a reputation for social responsibility protects firms from a decline in share prices associated with a crisis. Sauser, Jr. (2008) points to studies that found direct financial benefits for companies who are deemed to be socially responsible; and these benefits encompass enhanced business reputation, consumer acceptance, employee loyalty, as well as better environmental management. Hemlock (2007) reported on an academic analysis of dozens of corporate social responsibility studies that found that social responsibility performance and financial performance reinforce each other; that is, companies that excel in a socially responsible manner generally excel financially and vice versa. The aforementioned illustrations and studies demonstrate that social responsibility "pays off" for the company and its shareholders as well as for other stakeholders and society as a whole. *Business Week* (Engardio, 2007) reported one thought-provoking study that concluded that if Wal-Mart possessed the social responsibility reputation of its competitor, Target, Wal-Mart's stock would be worth 8.4% more, thereby adding $16 billion to its market capitalization.

The problem of determining if "doing good" translates to "doing well" is exacerbated since companies only report the value of tangible physical assets and investments in equipment and property. Social responsibility efforts are perhaps a bit too intangible for the company's accountants to quantify; and government regulators do not mandate that social responsibility, labor, and environmental practices be quantified. However, a company's commitment to social responsibility could constitute a valuable intangible business asset. Moreover, Spector (2012, p. 39) emphasizes that "tough global social issues are increasingly seen as responsibilities of businesses as well as governments, and innovative business leaders are viewing these problems as growth opportunities."

Social responsibility, therefore, though naturally possessing a religious element, is based predominantly on rationality; and thus excludes force – legal or otherwise - and even ethical or moral persuasion; rather, social responsibility in a global business context today relies on rationality and persuasion to adopt and "enforce" social responsibility standards and precepts. The characteristic "sanctions" in a societal environment that places value on "corporate social responsibility" encompass castigation, blame, criticism, negative publicity, loss of esteem, and disassociation, particularly for business in the form of employee recriminations and whistle-blowing, applicant avoidance, consumer boycotts, shareholder non- and disinvestment, as well as personal reactions such as anger, guilt, self-reproach, and remorse.

Although there is an expectation that business should be socially responsible, one implication, and potential problem for business, that has emerged is the permissible degree of pressure that a business can exert on its own employees to be socially responsible, especially when the demands entail the employee to spend his or her own money or personal time in charitable and civic-minded activities. Is it moral to pressure employees to be socially responsible? The good to the community might very well outweigh the "pain" in the form of expense and effort to the employees, and thus such "coercion" might be moral pursuant to Utilitarian ethics; but is the employee being treated as a mere "means" or instrument by his or her employer; and although for good ends, is the employee being so demeaned so as to make the employer's pressure immoral. Of course, if the employer is allowing its employees to be socially responsible on the company's time by encouraging them to participate in employer-sponsored volunteer programs, there should be no moral problem. Yet forcing employees to be socially responsible in addition to their work demands and workday duties can equate to unpaid and thus unethical overtime. Some employers will require such "volunteer" work, track the employees' time and efforts, and even assign the employee "volunteer" points on his or her performance evaluations. At the least, the employer should allow the employee, who very well may be very busy with a home life and personal commitments, to write a check to a charity as opposed to physically serving in a civic capacity. A better and more moral option, since it is not coercive, would be for the employer to encourage employees to be socially responsible, for example, by having a released-time program, for example, a "charity day," in which the employees would be released from work to volunteer for certain approved charities. The employees would have some flexibility in choosing their volunteer projects, and, most importantly, the employees would be paid by the company for their charity work (Banjo, 2009; Goodman, 2006; Alsop, 2002). Such programs would naturally benefit charity, treat the employees with respect, and, despite the expense, would benefit the employer in an egoistic sense in the long-run.

Another problem confronting corporate social responsibility, especially in the "constituency" or "sustainability" sense, is resistance from shareholders, who may be more interested in short-term profits than long-term sustainable profits. As explained by Millon (2011), "today's shareholders – particularly the large institutions that increasingly dominate the stock markets – typically prefer immediate maximization of share value over a more patient approach that is willing to wait for potentially greater returns in the future. This preference leads management to prioritize short-term profits over longer-run considerations. This approach obviously discourages constituency CSR because…benefits to nonshareholders reduce short-term profits and therefore have a negative impact on current share price" (p. 537). Nonetheless, it is the job of the business leader to educate the shareholders, and perhaps corporate management as well, of the benefits that will accrue to the company and the shareholders by the company acting in a smart, shrewd, and strategic socially responsible manner. Millon (2011) emphasizes that "the point is that investment in the well-being of key nonshareholder constituencies – even though costly in the short-run – can generate payoffs in the future that justify these expenditures" (p. 539). Harish (2012, p. 524) agrees, contending that "…corporate social responsibility can be of direct economic value. CSR should be treated as an investment, not a cost, much like quality improvement. They can thereby have an inclusive financial, commercial and social approach, leading to a long-term strategy minimizing risks linked to uncertainty." Similarly, and more strongly stated, Spector (2012, p. 44) declares: "posing shareholder and stakeholder interest as an either/or choice is a false dichotomy."

Business leaders, executives, and managers, as well as applicants for employment, therefore, must be cognizant of and appreciate the instrumental strategic value of social responsibility in its constituency and sustainability formulations. Business leaders, executives, and managers today surely are well aware of societal expectations regarding the social responsibility of their companies. Applicants for positions at these companies should be aware of social responsibility too. Yet applicants must be aware that companies very likely do not want a Ben & Jerry's expansive, but fiscally unrealistic and unsustainable, approach to social responsibility; but rather applicants who believe in, can define, and can implement a smart, shrewd, strategic, and ultimately sustainable approach to social responsibility. To illustrate, the recruitment manager for Timberland looks for M.B.A. job applicants that "who bring a passion for making the world a better place" and who have a "solid background" in corporate social responsibility, but the company does not want applicants who have "merely" taken academic courses in social responsibility, but students who have "gained practical experience related to social and environmental responsibility." Similarly, the Vice-President of Corporate Social Responsibility and Sustainability for Campbell Soup Co. indicated that the company is looking for employees who value social responsibility, but "...as a bottom-line booster, not just something to feel good about." The company, therefore, is looking, the V-P stated, not just for M.B.A.s who have studied the subject of social responsibility, but also those who can understand how to implement corporate social responsibility initiatives so that they can have a real impact and business connection. Accordingly, for job applicants today being socially responsible is a facet of having a good personal business sense as well as doing "good" for the firm and society as a whole.

Chapter 15

Stakeholder Values

Stakeholder theory was first developed over 40 years ago by Klaus Schwab, the founder and chairman of the World Economic Forum, based in Geneva, Switzerland. Schwab explained that "stakeholder theory…considers the enterprise as a community with a number of stakeholders – in other words, social groups that are directly and indirectly connected to the enterprise and that are dependent on its success and prosperity. These groups include employees, customers, suppliers, the state and especially the society's in which the enterprise is active" (Schwab, 2010, p. A19). In order to illustrate the stakeholders and values involved in business decision-making as well as to show the relationship among stakeholder values, social responsibility, and sustainability, the author has prepared the Table 15.1 for a quick review.

Table 15.1 shows the typical stakeholders in the business realm, that is, those constituent groups who are directly or indirectly affected by corporate actions. The Table then shows what these stakeholders value, that is, what they deem to possess worth - primarily and secondarily. These stakeholder groups typically are the following: shareholders and owners, employees, customers and consumers, suppliers and distributors, creditors, community, government, competition, and society. Shareholders as the "owners" of the corporate entity are always listed first.

Table 15.1 – Stakeholder Values,
Social Responsibility, and Sustainability

Stakeholders	Primary Values	Secondary Values
Owners / Shareholders	Financial Returns and Income	Growth and Added Value
Employees	Jobs and Pay	Job Stability and Satisfaction
Customers and Consumers	Supply of Goods and Services	Quality, Price, and Customer Service
Suppliers / Distributors	Contract Relationships and Payment	Long-term Relationships
Creditors	Payment and Rate of Return	Credit-worthiness and Security
Community	Employment and Tax-base	Philanthropy and Social Responsibility
Government	Legal Compliance and Tax-base	Competitiveness and Entrepreneurship
Competition	Market Share	Legal and Ethical Competition
Society	Growth, Prosperity, Sustainability	Social Responsibility and Environmental Stewardship and Improvement

Note: Table based on the Table – Stakeholders and Their Expectations - by Professor N. Harish (Harish, May 2012, p. 522), which Table was revised by the author for this book.

Obviously, a corporation cannot survive unless it serves and benefits its shareholders in a financial sense. However, today, shareholders may view their investment as one that benefits society too and perhaps in a direct manner by means of the social benefit corporation. Regardless, all shareholders are entitled to the honest and efficient management of their investment as well as a fair return on their investment. Employees, of course, are interested in obtaining and maintaining employment. They value a just wage, fair employment practices and working conditions, and job security. They also may value working for a company that is regarded as a "socially responsible" one. Customers and consumers want access to goods and services that are of good quality, at a fair price, and that come with good customer service. Suppliers and distributors want financially rewarding, long-term, contractual relationships with the company. Local communities want to see the corporation located in their cities and towns so as to provide employment for the citizens and residents and to support the local tax-base. The local community also values, and very well may expect, that the corporations in its presence participate in civic, charitable, philanthropic, and socially responsible activities. Creditors naturally value being repaid and also expect a fair rate of return as well as adequate assurances of security for the obligation. Government values legal compliance with business laws and business regulations. Government also values business as an important component of its tax-base. Government also values, and thus desires to promote, entrepreneurship and competition. As to the competition, the competition values its own market share, yet expects in a capitalistic model "tough" and "hard-hitting" competition, but the competition also values competition that is legal and ethical. Society values its survival, of course, and also growth, prosperity for its members, and the sustainability of business and society. Members of society also value today, and thus expect, that the corporation will be a socially responsible one, particularly regarding its stewardship of the environment and efforts to improve the environment.

The goal of the business leader today is to balance and harmonize these values and thus attempt to devise corporate policies that maximize these values in a legal, moral, socially responsible, and practically efficacious manner, thereby resulting in "win-win" scenarios for the business and all its stakeholders, and thereby attaining a level of continual sustainable business success.

Chapter 16

The Business Sustainability Continuum[7]

The term "sustainability" also has emerged, along with social responsibility and corporate governance, as important subject matters for business today. Paul (2012, p. 79) defines sustainability as follows: "A sustainable business is any organization that participates in environmentally friendly or green activities to ensure that all processes, products, and manufacturing activities adequately address current environmental concerns while maintaining a profit." Being a "green" business, moreover, means that a company is providing "environmentally friendly" services and products as well as one that has made "an enduring commitment to environmental principles in its business operations" (Paul, 2012, p. 79). The term, "The Triple Bottom Line," representing people, planet, and profits, which was created by John Elkington in 1994, also is directly related to sustainability. As explained by Paul (2012, p. 81): "It is a model or concept for compelling business leaders to consider more than just money. It requires business leaders and owners to balance social, financial, and environmental priorities. The Triple Bottom Line is sustainability – for the business world. The Triple Bottom Line grew out of a realization that we needed to find ways to do business without such a tremendous negative impact on the environment." According to Elkington, the three dimensions of sustainability under the "Triple P" formulation are economic prosperity, environmental quality, and social justice/equity. Sustainability has an ethical component and thus will result in ethical decision-making by companies. Moreover, Gupta

---

[7] Coauthored with Bahaudin G. Mujtaba, Nova Southeastern University.

(2012) asserts that consumers will consider the ethical implications of this decision-making and "...will have no qualms about boycotting products and corporations that do not act ethically" (p. 736).

A 2009 study of the views of chief executives, done by the Business Roundtable and the Conference Board, "...found that almost two-thirds indicated that sustainability has reached a tipping point and has become a mainstream concern for business (Spector, 2012, p. 41). An even larger 81% agreed that business leadership will increasingly be judged by the ability to create enterprises that are economically, socially, and environmentally sustainable" (Spector, 2012, p. 41). Furthermore, a 2011 IBM Institute for Business Value study, consisting of interviews at 320 global companies, "...concluded that today enterprise sustainability is a strategic imperative and 'no longer just a matter of legal compliance or philanthropic generosity'" (Spector, 2012, p. 42). Sherman (2012, p. 679) reports on a KPMG sustainability survey which "...found that 67% of G250 companies said that reputational or brand considerations were a driver for reporting, with ethical considerations (58%) also high on the list for sustainability reporting....Making the 'business case' for corporate social responsibility, 47% of the G250 felt their sustainability initiatives created financial value by increasing revenue, improving cost savings, or increasing market share." The United Nations also lists environmental sustainability as one of its Millennium Development Goals, along with reducing poverty, increasing education, promoting gender equality, improving child and maternal health, and combating HIV/AIDS. It is also possible now for a company to have a "sustainability" assessment. Moreover, an independent, international, private organization, the Global Reporting Initiative, based in Amsterdam and originating as part of a United Nations environmental program, has established Sustainability Reporting Guidelines, and has published assessment reports on a wide range of industries, including pharmaceutical, automotive, and consumer product industries. Gupta (2012) emphasizes that in this current age of "green washing," that is, making false or misleading claims about a company be environmentally friendly, it is critical that companies utilize sustainability standards and provide sustainability information that are clear and verifiable and thus that the consumers can trust. Sherman (2012, p. 675) also addresses the problem of "all the inconsistency in defining and measuring sustainability"; but points out that "the most widely recognized guidelines for the reporting of economic, environmental, and social performance were developed by the Global Reporting Initiative (GRI)." The GRI *Guidelines* have 79 performance indicators, fifty of which are deemed to be "core"; some are quantitative, such as greenhouse gas emissions by weight, whereas others are qualitative, such as community impact. Sherman (2012, p. 676) also notes that "while compliance with the GRI's *Guidelines* is entirely voluntary, more than 1800 reports were officially registered with the GRI in 2012."

Sustainability, of course, encompasses legal, ethical, moral, and social responsibility values; and sustainability is related to corporate governance. Furthermore, social entrepreneurship is directly related to sustainability because "a social entrepreneur, similar to a business entrepreneur, builds strong and sustainable organizations" (p. 50) based on "sustainability models" and well-elaborated feasibility studies (p. 51). However, as Spector (2012, p. 42) correctly points out, dealing with sustainability may be a difficult challenge for certain business executives: "One of the causes may be that the sustainability aim of creating long-term value, while balancing the business need for profit with the ethics of social and environmental responsibility, is uncharged territory for traditional compliance-oriented corporate governance practice."

Spector (2012, p. 44) posits there are three common "misconceptions" about sustainability; and he offers corresponding "corrective actions," to wit: The first misconception is that many corporate leaders feel that sustainability is an increasingly popular notion, but it is an "essentially unknown business concept"; but Spector advises that business leaders must understand sustainability and concomitantly must be aware that there exists a substantial body of literature on sustainability, and thus business leaders must begin to discuss the application of sustainability to specific situations involving their companies. The second misconception is that many business people believe that sustainability decisions are financially unsound and will harm the shareholders; but Spector (2012) advises that the corrective action is for business leaders to realize that "the case of financial and competitive benefits of pursuing an aggressive sustainability strategy," and thus business leaders should "conduct a thorough assessment of the opportunities for improving sustainability and advancing business goals" (p. 44). Finally, the third misconception is the belief by corporate board leaders that allocating resources to sustainability initiatives is a violation of the duty to maximize shareholder wealth; but Spector (2012) maintains that the traditional "business judgment rule" of corporate law will protect consideration of other stakeholder interests in an effort to promote shareholder value (p. 44). Spector (2012, p. 44) concludes that regarding sustainability, "posing shareholder and stakeholder interest as an either/or choice is a false dichotomy." Paul (2012, p. 82) provides a similar "instrumental" rationale for sustainability as a "management philosophy," to wit: "For companies, it's no longer good enough to focus only on the financial bottom line. Companies must invest on the social and environmental fronts as well, not only because it's the right thing to do, but for business reasons. Poor performance in the social and environmental areas will ultimately infect financial performance and shareholder value."

In order to better illustrate as well as explicate the values of practicality, legality, morality, social responsibility, and stakeholder interests, and their relationship to sustainability, the authors have developed a sustainability model, called The Business Sustainability Continuum (BSC); see Figure 16.1.

The BSC illustrates that the continual success and "sustainability" of the business can only be achieved by an adherence to four core values: *Economic*, indicating that a business obviously must have a viable business model which fulfills a need and enables the business to make a profit; *Legal*, indicating that this profit must be achieved in legal manner by aligning the conduct of the business with all applicable local, national, and international law; *Ethical*, indicating that since there may be no law or "gaps" in the law, nonetheless the business must act in a moral manner and also must act in conformity with its values, promises, and obligations; and *Social Responsibility*, indicating that the business must focus on the community and engage prudently in civic, philanthropic, and charitable endeavors as part of the business' overall strategic plan. Sustainability will help the business; but also help the business help governments solve pressing social problems, and, as such, "this provides an occasion to rebuild trust that is good for business and good for society" (Spector, 2012, p. 39). Harish (2012, p. 521) adds that "CSR has been widely regarded as a positive phenomenon helping bridge the gap of social inequality and thus contributing to sustainable development."

Figure 16.1 - The Business Sustainability Continuum (BSC)

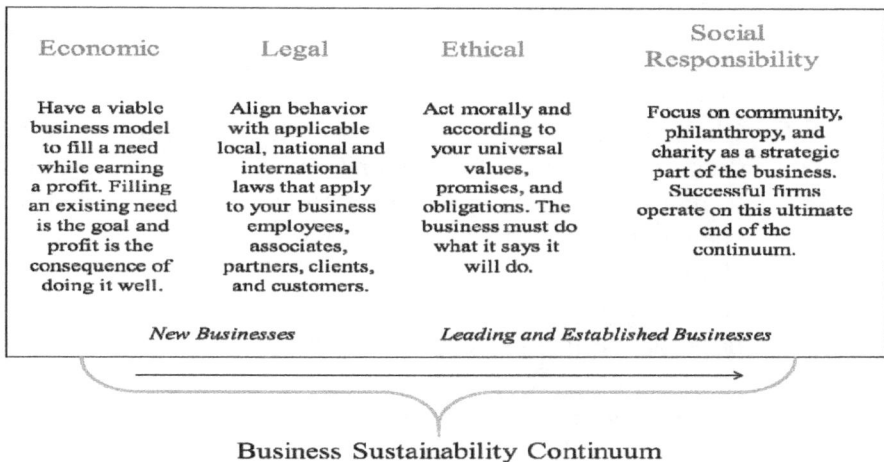

Economic	Legal	Ethical	Social Responsibility
Have a viable business model to fill a need while earning a profit. Filling an existing need is the goal and profit is the consequence of doing it well.	Align behavior with applicable local, national and international laws that apply to your business employees, associates, partners, clients, and customers.	Act morally and according to your universal values, promises, and obligations. The business must do what it says it will do.	Focus on community, philanthropy, and charity as a strategic part of the business. Successful firms operate on this ultimate end of the continuum.
New Businesses		*Leading and Established Businesses*	

Business Sustainability Continuum

However, too much of focus on the "strategic" (that is, "bottom-line" centered) nature of social responsibility may cause companies to lose track of the broader, stakeholder, societal notion of social responsibility. Accordingly, adherence to, as well as prudence in the implementation of, these "sustainable" values will enable the business to achieve success and to sustain that success in a continual manner, thereby benefiting the business, its shareholders, the communities where it does business, and all the stakeholders affected by the business, including society as a whole.

Strategic thinking should also be focused on sustainable planning. According to Barry Barnes, "in today's fast-changing world, there's a huge demand for capable and effective leaders all around the globe. In all modern organizations, we look for executives who can successfully lead it to a sustainable future. So what we need today are effective leaders at all levels of our organizations, whether they are executives, managers or simply informal leaders" (Barnes, 3013, para. 1). Barnes continues to say that effective leaders need to do following on a regular basis:

1. Articulate an inspiring vision of the future.
2. Lead by example. Walk the talk. And remember that you're always leading by example whether you realize it or not.
3. Be trustworthy and create trust with followers.
4. Have high expectations for followers. Setting the bar high will motivate followers to grow and achieve more...especially if it's linked to rewards.
5. Challenge the process. Recognize that "the way we've always done things around here" won't always allow the organization to reach a common goal. As a result, be ready and willing to change the system and engage followers in the process of change.
6. Adjust your style to meet follower needs. As followers improve performance, adjust your leadership style to move from telling followers what to do, to mentoring and persuading them, then to encouraging and facilitating their actions, and finally to simply entrusting them and monitoring their progress (Barnes, 2013, para. 5).

Luckily, today successful leaders and managers are found at all levels of modern organizations. As per the essence of the Business Sustainability Continuum and regardless of our position in the organization, let us all become responsible employees, professionals, managers, leaders, and executives who can think strategically and lead ourselves, our organizations, and the society toward a sustainable future.

Chapter 17

Motivations for Social and Environmental Responsibility[8]

The late Ray Anderson, founder of the multinational flooring corporation Interface, transformed his company's way of working into one that was clearly not "business as usual." He launched a plan, called "Mission Zero," to eliminate any negative impact the company may have on the environment by the year 2020 through the redesign of processes and products, the pioneering of new technologies, and efforts to reduce or eliminate waste and harmful emissions while increasing the use of renewable materials and sources of energy. Howard Schulz, founder of Starbucks, in negotiating with East African coffee bean growers, insisted that a key condition for purchasing from their cooperatives was that they establish systems for health insurance and education for members of their cooperatives. These were families he would never meet; and when the initiative was first implemented, it was not even advertised in any of Starbucks' corporate PR campaigns.

Have you ever wondered why some corporate leaders decide to champion social or environmentally positive initiatives, even when it is not part of their formal role, and no one has asked them to do so? And especially when it may even demand of them a great effort to have to defend their unusual way of running their business? That was my question a few years ago, because I thought that if we understood the key factors prompting those atypical managers to action, we might

---

[8] Contributed by Isabel Rimanoczy, Legacy Coach.

find guidance in how to intentionally develop the next generation of leaders.

Introduction

Inspired by this question I focused my doctoral research on sixteen business leaders that championed sustainability initiatives, seeking to understand why they did so, what they knew, how they thought, and what motivated or inspired them. The leaders worked in a variety of industries, were all in higher leadership roles (VP, Director, CEO, Founder) that gave them influence and decision-making power; and they all had in common the fact that they had each made the personal decision to champion initiatives that made a positive impact on the social or environmental conduct of the corporation. They had not been invited or asked to do so, and, as a matter of fact, had to endure great resistance and internal challenges to pursue their projects (See Table 1 with the demographics of the group).

The Findings

Although previous research efforts had addressed CSR initiatives of different sorts, they concentrated mostly on the technical aspects of the projects, and there was little data about personal motivation, or about the constellation of factors that could influence a person to choose that 'least traveled path' in a business environment ruled by short term ROI's, shareholders, and size of market share. This was uncharted territory; and so the study was designed as a qualitative, exploratory research of sixteen exemplary individuals. I focused on identifying what forces prepared them to take action--meaning the factors that led up to their intentional acts within the scope of CSR; what their learning strategies were, since this was a new area for all of them; what their implementation tactics were; and what mindset or personal attitudes they found helpful-- or less so.

While the number of leaders interviewed was not meant to be a representative sample, nonetheless, the study surfaced interesting information. They were influenced by a wide spectrum of factors-- ranging from personal trigger events, transformational experiences or encounters, their personal upbringing, role models and influential mentors, and differing weight of a sense of personal mission or spiritual practices, but I was able to further identify three main factors that occurred in sequence and that had great impact on the leaders.

Table 17.1 - Demographics of the Individuals Studied

Name	Gender		Industrial area	Age	Position	Currently
	M	F				
Anthony	x		Retail	75	CEO-Founder, medium size US multinational corporation (MNC)	Chairman and speaker
Jack	x		Technology	70	Former VP Product Development, large US MNC	Faculty
Raul	x		Technology	66	Former CEO, small US MNC	Transitioning to a new job connected with sustainability
Stephen	x		Food	61	Chairman, large US corporation	Retiring, starting a major philanthropic initiative
Harry	x		NGO	60	President-Founder- association of corporations, NGOs and government	same
Malcolm	x		Household products	56	VP, medium size US corporation	Corporate Social Consciousness Director
Diego	x		Coffee	56	President-Founder, small US corporation	same
Howard	x		Apparel	53	Director, medium size US corporation	same
Kevin	x		Pharmaceutical	53	VP, large European MNC	same
Ronald	x		Restaurant	53	Global Senior VP, large US MNC	same
Daisy		x	Apparel	53	Former Global Director Research, Design and Development, large US MNC	Starting Sustainability consulting firm
Shani		x	Food	49	Director, Legal Affairs, large US MNC	same
Barry	x		Coffee Coop	47	President, Founder small international Cooperative	same
Stanley	x		Restaurant	45	Former President and Owner of large US Franchises-in Europe	CEO/Founder of a sustainability investment fund
Janine		x	Food	39	VP, R&D, large European MNC	same
Nelson	x		Food	37	VP, Investors Relations, large US corporation	same

CEO: Chief Executive Officer. VP: Vice President. R&D: Research and Development

The "Whack on the Head"

In a variety of circumstances, the individuals I studied were exposed to information about the 'state of the planet." Independently of how this occurred, what I repeatedly found was that at some point they were faced with data that they had not been aware of before; data that gave them a broader picture of the planetary situation in areas such as the extent of industrial contamination of waterways and chemical alteration of underground water; the volume of water used in industry and the increasing percentage of populations who lacked safe drinking water; the soil contamination due to petroleum-based fertilizers and pesticides, and loss of soil nutrients due to monocultures in industrial farming; the greenhouse gas emissions and climate consequences; the social and economic gap due to an increasing migration into urban concentrations, and subsequent loss of community bonds; the depletion of forests; the removal of mountain tops for mining purposes the loss of biodiversity; the growing extinction of registered species of flora and fauna; the use of nature as a resource without attention paid to the replenishment conditions; and the use of chemicals and genetically modified organisms whose effects we ignore.

I include verbatim comments of several interviewees in which they describe their individual reactions to what they experienced:

> I noticed the smell; I mean, the chemicals that are used when you stick things together [...] they're very toxic. [...] It was hot and there was this one woman on the line working with this chemical, visibly pregnant. I asked my interpreter to ask her whether or not the smell bothered her. And her answer sticks with me to this day. She said only on Sundays, which is the one day they don't work. That was the day she would have headaches. [...] a wake-up call that there is such huge disparity in the world. I think that's when I really started to be extremely active and vocal around diversity and inclusion and equity. (Daisy)

On about page 19, I came to this chapter heading, "The Death of Birth," and I began to read. I very quickly found out what the death of birth was. Of course, it was species' extinction, species disappearing, never, ever again to experience the miracle of birth, and it was like a spear in the chest, because Hawken, within 20 pages, he had made this case.

'The living systems of earth are in decline, leading to species extinction. The culprit – the biggest culprit in this decline is the industrial system that takes from the earth, makes stuff that ends up as waste in the landfill or an incinerator very quick in a take, make, waste linear system. It's destroying the biosphere, and, yeah, when you look at that problem, there's only one institution on earth that has the solution to the problem. It's the same one that created the problem, because the institution of business and industry is the largest. It is the wealthiest. It is the most pervasive and the most influential institution on earth, and it's the culprit in this, so only it has the power to change all of that.'

Well, I took that message in. I took it in really, really seriously… (Anthony)

We are now certainly receiving reports daily in the media about weather-related problems or catastrophes, about social and economic disparity and its consequences, and about threatened species or rainforests. What we rarely see, though, is all the pieces of this complex puzzle put together. This is something that I observed in several of the business leaders studied, and that I also later confirmed among MBA students and business leaders who have participated in my workshops.

'This week's readings and videos were shocking. Not only they opened my eyes more on how everything is not ok, but also showed me how bad things really are and

how I am part of it even when I try to be as eco-friendly
as possible. It is amazing to see how we are continuously
ruining our environment and how everything is coming to
an end.' (Alejandra)

It seems that by seeing the larger picture we are also "seeing the
forest" that we otherwise miss as we pursue our long lists of daily
obligations. The effect of this fuller picture is what I liken to a
"whack in the head."

The "Squeeze of the Heart"

While we tend to connect with reality through our "left brain"
hemisphere, i.e., analyzing, measuring, seeking numbers and facts,
creating logical connections and trying to stay objective and rational,
this is not what was discovered in my study. Quite to the contrary, I
found that the "whack in the head," the cognitive and intellectual
acknowledgment of facts, was immediately followed by strong
emotions:

> …and I would read passages in bed at night to my wife,
> and we would weep together over the plight of the earth,
> and I was part of the problem. I was part of this
> industrial system that's destroying the biosphere. The
> living systems and the life support systems of earth are in
> decline partially because of me, and by this time I had
> grandchildren, you see. So when I read the book and had
> this overwhelming emotional response to it, like a spear
> in the chest, the point of that spear touched my soul.
> (Anthony)

> I'll never forget as long as I live the feeling I had after his
> first two hours, because I was ready to shoot myself. I
> mean, I was literally—I've never been more suicidal in
> my life. It was so depressing what he told me that I was
> literally distraught. (Stanley)

> I'd always kind of known that we were out there doing things, but it was, I was probably just busy doing my day job, and I didn't worry too much about it [...] It's sort of embarrassing when I look back to think how little energy I sort of put into it. [...] I think, if anything, I feel guilty sometimes because I don't do enough...(Janine)

Feelings were mentioned in one way or another by each one of the sixteen individuals. Seven participants mentioned pain, sadness, despair, or depression. Six individuals expressed feelings akin to anger, something "driving them crazy," or feeling rebellious. The language was very emphatic: Jack talked about "what blows my mind," Raul mentioned "a deep fire in my belly and deep anger about just how foolish human beings are in the aggregate."

The immediate impact of information on the heart, on personal values, and on their personal contribution to the problem, was something I have also observed among MBA students and in leadership workshops:

> This video is amazing. What's more amazing is the embarrassment/shame I feel for humans [...] I particularly am pointing to our sustainability class because as I reflect back on my 27 year life, I wonder what I did in life to help the environment. Am I just another contributor to the worst disease for this world? Major change is needed in my life... (Rabih)

> The reading from this week truly frightened me within the first several pages, especially the theory that life could become totally unsustainable within forty years. Forty! I don't know about you, but I can't surrender to that notion. In a way, that fact frightens, enlightens, discourages and encourages me all at the same time. (Matthew)

Stanley described it this way: "So having seen all of that, I just looked inside of me, and I said, 'What can I do?'"

Feelings played a major role as triggers to action, which takes us to the third key source of impact.

The "Hands in Action"

As a way to deal with their strong emotions, the business leaders in my study felt the urge to take action. Some were aware of the responsibility of their leadership position in responding to the problems they witnessed: "Maybe my job is to lift the veil to everybody, and have them open and see" (Shani). Some realized they knew something others still ignored and had to share it:

> I said that we were gonna become a learning organization and that [...] a cornerstone would be that we would learn about sustainability, and that I would take everyone through this education process. (Raul)

Still others felt privileged to have the talents and skills that they wanted to use in a positive way. Whatever the reason, they all needed to act.

They knew that dissemination of information was essential if they were going to be successful in inducing change, and so they started by sharing all they knew with others – peers and bosses as well as direct reports. Instinctively they attempted to replicate the sequence of experiences that they had gone through, but with a slight difference. In their own awakening, they had not focused on responding in a rational, business-oriented manner. However, in considering how best to bring the necessary awareness to their leadership colleagues, they decided that they had to do it through presenting a "business case." They went to great lengths to identify savings opportunities, and the potential economic benefits that would accrue, as a means to rationalize why something had to change in the way they were doing business. This approach, ironically, was not the one that had moved them to action, because it was not the profitability of a business case that had so passionately moved them. For them, it had been the emotional impact of a "whack on the head."

Some realized this when they addressed their colleagues or leaders had described and showed how they had been convinced, for instance, by showing a full picture of the damage we as humanity are inflicting on our planet, and helping explore the feelings this generated. One leader took a large group of executives to a landfill, to observe for the first time what was laying there. In another case, a group was taken to a forest, and asked to reflect in silence about what their role in life was.

One CEO expressed his astonishment when he organized a town-hall meeting to share with the employees the information he had learned. "They immediately jumped on it, they were so passionate and we had to put certain restrictions to the suggestions because we were flooded with initiatives and ideas on what to do differently, in an environmental and socially responsible way."

Summary

So what does this story tell us? It tells me that we may be collectively short-changing ourselves if we behave solely in a rational, objective, and "cool" way; we must also be guided by our emotional reactions and respond to the feelings that emerge strongly in our heart. We are born with a need for meaning; we seek purpose, and it is not found in consumption, in higher returns of our savings, or even in the invention of the next gadget. Deep inside, we all know that, but somehow we assume that it is not something valid for others as well, that it is just our personal preference and not something other people would share. We assume that the "real world" is the world of numbers and profits, and that making strictly rational decisions is how to manage our life. I am not advocating for irrational decisions, but perhaps the picture of what our Earth looks like, after a few hundred years of very "rational" decisions, suggests that we may review what "rationality" means. Consider this: water, air, soil, food, other human beings, every single thing we depend on comes from nature and cannot be manufactured by all our human ingenuity. Adopting social and environmentally responsible behaviors may be something that feels deeply right, and may also result in being a good, rational, business decision.

Chapter 18

Conclusion

One can argue philosophically whether values are "real" intrinsically; yet it would seem beyond reasonable dispute that values possess instrumental worth. Values today increasing drive consumer and also employee behavior. Consumers will want to do business with, and employees will want to work for, employers whose values are compatible. Legality, ethics, and morality are very important values; and today social responsibility is such a value too. Business leaders must be cognizant of these values. Furthermore, the emphasis on stakeholders or constituency groups is an essential component of business leadership today too. The business leader must take an enlightened approach to satisfying the values of stakeholders in order to achieve long-term sustainable success. As emphasized, the ultimate goal is to attain "win-win" resolutions whereby all the company's stakeholders receive value. Social responsibility emerges as a key element in achieving stakeholder symmetry, business success, and business sustainability. Furthermore, given the apparent positive relationship between successful financial performance and social responsibility, and the critical need of both these values for society and the economic system, corporate social responsibility has emerged as a most relevant and profound topic for business today.

Social responsibility, moreover, now is not "just" an "academic" matter for business school students, or "merely" an "issue" for social activists; rather, social responsibility is also a very real and practical concern for the global business leader, executive, manager and entrepreneur. Admittedly, in certain cases, social responsibility concerns may be more difficult for business people, who are primarily focused on economic issues, to discern and to handle. Moreover, there may be conflicts as various constituencies make conflicting demands. Nonetheless, business leaders are expected to recognize competing stakeholder interests, to provide balance among legitimate competing claims, and, as emphasized, to devise practical, legal, ethical, socially responsible, as well as mutually beneficial solutions. Business leaders very well may have to convince certain stakeholders, such as the shareholders, that it is in their long-term self-interest to accept some short-term financial sacrifice, say in the form of company socially responsible efforts in the local community, in order to produce long-term greater financial gains. Fundamentally, therefore, business leaders are expected to lead, and to lead by values, encompassing legal values, moral values, and now today socially responsible values too. Consequently, cognizance of, adherence to, and successfully dealing with the value of social responsibility have become imperatives for business leaders today.

Modern business leaders must recognize that social responsibility and sustainability are now essential aspects of business; and thus these values must have a prominent place on the corporate vision, mission, and agenda. The view today is that business should pursue profits, of course, but also that business should strive to achieve social objectives too in sustainable manner. Business leaders should, and actually are expected to, know and understand the rationales for corporate social responsibility and business sustainability as well as are expected to create and implement corporate strategies to be a socially responsible and sustainable business. Social responsibility as well as sustainability, therefore, should now be incorporated into business values, missions, and models. Social responsibility is the now the modern way, and truly the only sustainable way, to do business. However, as the author and contributors have emphasized throughout this book, social responsibility clearly possesses instrumental value because it can be used in a smart, shrewd, and strategic sense to help the business achieve and sustain successful performance. Social responsibility, therefore, is more than "mere" "pure" charity; rather, in modern business sense social responsibility is an integral strategic component in a company's endeavor to achieve larger business objectives; and concomitantly, and also propitiously, society as whole is benefitted too by these social responsibility activities. Business, therefore, needs a formal, coherent, transparent, strategic, stakeholder-based, and sustainable policy of social responsibility. The goal is to make a positive, beneficial, and sustainable contribution to the company's fiscal growth, overall economic growth, societal growth and development, and the betterment of the environment. So, corporate social responsibility and sustainability are "smart business" and "good business" – for business and society. The old maxim is true: one can do well by doing "good"!

Bibliography

Afsharipour, Afra (Summer, 2011). Directors as Trustees of the Nation? India's Corporate Governance and Corporate Social Responsibility. *Seattle University Law Review*, Vol. 34, pp. 995-1024.

Abuznaid, S. (2006), 'Islam and management: What can be learned?', *Thunderbird International Business Review*, Vol. 48, No. 1

Ali, Imran (2013). How Corporate Social Responsibility and Corporate Reputation Influence Employee Engagement. Unpublished manuscript.

Ali, I.; Rehman, K. U.; and Akram, M. (2011). Corporate social responsibility and investor satisfaction influences on investor loyalty. *Actual Problems of Economics*, 8(122):348-357.

Ali, A.J. (2008), 'Islamic work ethic: A critical review', *Cross Cultural Management: an International Journal*, Vol. 18, No.1.

Alsop, Ronald (January 16, 2002). Perils of Corporate Philanthropy. *The Wall Street Journal*, pp. B1, B4.

Alsop, Ronald (December 13, 2005). Recruiters Seek M.B.As Trained in Responsibility. *The Wall Street Journal*, p. B6.

American Law Institute (1994). 1 *Principles of Corporate Governance*, Section 2.01.

Anderson, R.C. (2000). *Mid-course correction. Toward a Sustainable Enterprise: The Interface Model*. Chelsea Green Publishing.

Andre, Rae (2012). Assessing the Accountability of the Benefit Corporation: Will This New Gray Sector Organization Enhance Corporate Social Responsibility? *Journal of Business Ethics*, Vol. 110, pp. 133-150.

Armstrong, M (2009). Handbook of Human Resource Management Practice,. Kogan Page Limited, UK

Banjo, Shelly (January 14, 2009). Next Benefit to Face Ax: Matching Gifts. *The Wall Street Journal*, pp. D1, D3.

Barnes, B. (August 19, 2013). *Six Lessons for 21st Century Leaders*. H. Huizenga School of Business and Entrepreneurship blog, Nova Southeastern University . Retrieved on August 20, 2013 from: http://www.huizenga.nova.edu/faculty-blog/

Barney, J. and Wright, P. (1998). On becoming strategic partner: the role of human resources in gaining competitive advantage. *Human Resource Management*, vol. 37

Barney, J. (1995). Looking inside for competitive advantage. *Academy of Management Executive*, vol. 9: 49-61

Bauerlein, Valerie (January 21, 2011). Pepsi Hits "Refresh" on Donor Project. *The Wall Street Journal*, p. B4.

Becker, B.E., and Huselid, M.A., Pickus, P.S. and Spratt, M.F. (1997). HR as a
source of shareholder values: research and recommendations. *Human
Resource Management,* 36 (1).

Becker, B.E. and Huselid, M.A. (1998). High Performance Work Systems and Firm
Performance: a synthesis of research and managerial implications.
Research in Personnel and Human Resources, vol. 16.

Bondy, Krista, Moon, Jeremy, and Matten, Dirk (2012). An Institution of Corporate
Social Responsibility (CSR) in Multi-National Corporations (MNCs).
Journal of Business Ethics, Vol. 111, pp. 281-299.

Brady, Diane (November 12-18, 2012). Volunteerism as a Core Competency.
Bloomberg Businessweek, pp. 53-54.

Brennan, John J. (May 10, 2010). Improving Corporate Governance: A Memo to the
Board. *The Wall Street Journal,* p. A7.

Business Briefing (March 4, 2006). Wal-Mart to hire ethics watchdog. *Sun-Sentinel,*
p. B1.

Business Briefing (October 26, 2011). Coke adds white, and also bears. *Sun-
Sentinel,* p. 3D.

Bussey, John (October 28, 2011). Are Companies Responsible for Creating Jobs?
The Wall Street Journal, pp. B1, B2.

Cahyandito, Martha Fani (March 2012). Corporate Social Responsibility into
Millennium Development Goals is a Mere Wishful Thinking? *Journal of
Management and Sustainability,* Vol. 2, No. 1, pp. 67-86.

Cavico, F. J. and Mujtaba, B. G. (2014). Social Responsibility, Stakeholders,
Sustainability, and Corporate Governance. Chapter 3, pp. 31-64. In
Governance in Action Globally – Strategy, Processes and Reality, by Rossi
Smith, Academic Publishers.

Cavico, F. J. and Mujtaba, B. G. (August 15, 2013). Health and Wellness Policy
Ethics. *International Journal of Health Policy and Management,* 1(2), 111-
113.

Cavico, F. J. and Mujtaba, B. G. (2012a). National and Global Perspectives of
Corporate Social Responsibility. *International Journal of Management
Sciences and Business Research,* 1(3), pp. 1-24.

Cavico, F. J. and Mujtaba, B. G. (2012b). Social Responsibility, Corporate
Constituency Statutes, and the Social Benefit Corporation. *International
Journal of Management and Administrative Sciences,* 1(7), pp. 21-25.

Cavico, F. J. and Mujtaba, B. G. (2009). *Business Ethics: The Moral Foundation of
Effective Leadership, Management, and Entrepreneurship* (Second
Edition). New York: Pearson Custom Publishing.

Cavico, F. J. and Mujtaba, B. G. (2008). *Legal Challenges for the Global Manager
and Entrepreneur.* Dubuque, Iowa: Kendall-Hunt Publishing Company.

Chandler, David L. (2012, January 30). *For businesses, going green brings in
greenbacks.* Retrieved from Massachusetts Institute of Technology News
website: http://web.mit.edu/newsoffice/2012/manufacturing-green-
0130.html

Chatterji, Aaron K., and Richman, Barak D. (Summer, 2008). Understanding the "Corporate" in Corporate Social Responsibility. *Harvard Law and Policy Review*, Vol. 2, pp. 33-48.

Christopher, John, and Bernhart, Michelle (Fall 2009). Communicate our Values: Social Responsibility as a Recruitment and Retention Strategy. *HR Florida Review*, pp. 8-12.

Chu, Kathy (April 19, 2012). Apple may polish China image. *USA Today*, p. 9A.

Clark, William H., and Babson, Elizabeth K. (2012). Business Organizations: When "Business Purpose" Disappears; How Benefit Corporations are Redefining the Purpose of Business Organizations. *William Mitchell Law Review*, Vol. 38, pp. 817-844).

Cohen, Rodgin H. and Schleyer, Glen T. (2012). Shareholder vs. Director Control Over Social Policy Matters: Conflicting Trends in Corporate Governance. *Notre Dame Journal of Law, Ethics, & Public Policy*, Vol. 26, pp. 81-124.

Cone, Tracie (October 15, 2009). IHOP egg production under fire. *Sun-Sentinel*, p. 3D.

Conlin, Michelle (November 27, 2006). More Micro, Less Soft. *Business Week*, p. 42.

Conlin, Michelle, and Hempel, Jessi (December 1, 2003). Philanthropy 2003: The Corporate Donors. *Business Week*, pp. 92-96.

Cordle, Ina Paiva (June 7, 2012). Entrepreneurs aim higher than bottom line. *Miami Herald*, pp. 1A, 5A.

Cummings, Briana (April 2012). Benefit Corporations: How to Enforce a Mandate to Promote the Public Interest. *Columbia Law Review*, Vol. 112, pp. 578-661.

Daniel, Trenton (October 22, 2010). New School, new hope for young Haitians. *The Miami Herald*. Retrieved October 22, 2010 from: http://www.miamiherald.com/2010/10/22/v-print/18885560/new-school-new-hope-for-young-haitians.

Delaney, Kevin J. (January 18, 2008). Google: From "Don't be Evil" to How to Do Good. *The Wall Street Journal*, pp. B1, B2.

Delaney, Kevin J. (October 12, 2005). Google Outlines Philanthropic Plan. *The Wall Street Journal*, p. B5.

De Roeck, Kenneth, and Delobber, Nathalie (2012). Do Environmental CSR Initiatives Serve Organizations' Legitimacy in the Oil Industry? Exploring Employees' Reactions Through Organizational Identification Theory. *Journal of Business Ethics*, Vol. 110(4), pp. 397-412.

Deskins, Michael R. (Winter, 2011). Benefit Corporation Legislation, Version 1.0 – A Breakthrough in Stakeholder Rights. *Lewis & Clark Law Review*, Vol. 15, pp. 1047-1076.

Dizik, Alina (march 4, 2010). Social Concerns Gain New Urgency. *The Wall Street Journal*, p. B10.

Du, Shullii, and Verira, Edward T. (2012). Striving for Legitimacy Through Corporate Social Responsibility: Insights from Oil Companies. *Journal of Business Ethics*, Vol. 110(4), pp. 413-427.

Eabrasu, Marian (2012). A Moral Pluralist Perspective on Corporate Social Responsibility: From Good to Controversial Practices. *Journal of Business Ethics*, Vol. 110(4), pp. 429-439.

Editorials (September 11, 2000). New Economy, New Social Contract. *Business Week*, p. 182.

Engardio, Pete (January 29, 2007). Beyond the Green Corporation. *Business Week*, pp.50-64.

EPA Green Power Partnership. (2013). *Fortune 500 Partners List.* Retrieved from http://www.epa.gov/greenpower/toplists/fortune500.htm

Executive Suite (February 6, 2006). A Social Strategist For Wal-Mart. *Business Week*, p. 11.

Flint, Joe, Branch, Shelly, and O'Connell, Vanessa (December 14, 2001). Breaking Longtime Taboo, NBC Network Plans to Accept Liquor Ads. *The Wall Street Journal*, pp. B1, B6.

Florida Statutes Section 607.083(3) (2011).

Foreman, Ellen (October 27, 1996). Businesses told they can be ethical and profitable. *Sun-Sentinel*, pp. 1G, 2G.

Fox, Adrienne (August 2007). Corporate Social Responsibility Pays Off. *HR Magazine*, pp. 43-47.

Garcia, Jason (September 30, 2009). 1 Million Volunteers to Visit Disney for Free. *Sun-Sentinel*, Money, pp. 1-2.

Gelter, Martin (Spring, 2011). Taming or Protecting the Modern Corporation? Shareholder – Stakeholder Debates in a Comparative Light. *New York University Journal of Law & Business*, Vol. 7, pp. 641-740.

George, Bill (September 13-19, 2010). Executive Pay: Rebuilding Trust in an Era of Rage. *Bloomberg Businessweek*, p. 56.

Givray, Henry S. (September 3, 2007). When CEOs Aren't Leaders. *Business Week*, p. 102.

GlaxoSmithKline (2005). Corporate Responsibility Report 2005. Retrieved January 28, 2007 from: http://www.gsk.com/respnsibility/cr_report_2005.

Goodman, Cindy Krischer (November 8, 2006). Volunteering through work isn't always so voluntary. *The Miami Herald*, pp. 1C, 5C.

Gore, Al and Blood, David (July 24, 2010). Toward Sustainable Capitalism. *The Wall Street Journal*, p. 21.

Gupta, Atul (July/August, 2012). Sustainable Competitive Advantage in Service Corporations. *The Journal of Applied Business Research*, Vol. 28, No. 4, pp.735-42.

Guthrie, W.K.C. (1988). *The Sophists*. Great Britain: Cambridge University Press.

Hai-yan, He, Amerzaga, Teodoro Rafael Wendlandt, and Silva, Beatriz Ochoa (March 2012). Corporate Social Responsibility Perspectives and Practices in Chinese Companies: A Brief Overview on Environment, Consumers and

External Communication. *Journal of Management and Sustainability*, Vol. 2, No. 1, pp. 57-86.

Harish, N. (May 2012). Corporate Social Responsibility Practices in Indian Companies: A Study. International Journal of Management, IT and Engineering, Vol. 2, Issue 5, pp. 519-36.

Harrington, Alexandra R. (2011/2012). Protecting Workers' Rights in a Post-Wisconsin World: Strategies for Organizing and Action in an Era of Diminished Resources and Embattled Unions: Corporate Social Responsibility, Globalization, the Multinational Corporation, and Labor: An Unlikely Alliance. *Albany Law Review*, Vol. 75, pp. 481-508.

Hasnas, John (2013). Whiter Stakeholder Theory? A Guide for the Perplexed Revisited. *Journal of Business Ethics*, Vol. 112, pp. 47-57.

Haymore, Steven J. (May, 2011). Publicly Oriented Companies: B Corporations and the Delaware Stakeholder Provision Dilemma. *Vanderbilt Law Review*, Vo. 64, pp. 1311-1342.

Heineman, Jr., Ben W. (June 28, 2005). Are You a Good Corporate Citizen? *The Wall Street Journal*, p. B2.

Hemlock, Doreen (March 11, 2007). It's all good: Social awareness now a corporate requirement. *Sun-Sentinel,* Business and Money, pp. 1E, 2E.

Hempel, Jessi, and Gard, Lauren (November 29, 2004). Philanthropy 2004: The Corporate Donors. *Business Week*, pp. 100-104.

Higgens, Alexander G. (June 21, 2001). Coca-Cola to join AIDs fight in Africa. *The Miami Herald*, p. 4C.

Hiltrop, J.M. (1995). The changing psychological contract: the human resource challenge of the 1990s. *European Management Journal, vol. 13, No. 3*

Holme, Lord and Watts, Richard (2004). Making Good Business Sense. *The World Business Council for Sustainable Development.*

Homes, Stanley (September 9, 2002). For Coffee Growers, Not Even a Whiff of Profits. *Business Week*, p. 110.

Horney, K. (1951). Neurosis and Human Growth: The Struggle Toward Self-Realization. London: Routledge and Kegan Paul

Jacobs, Michael (April 24, 2009). How Business Schools Have Failed Business. *The Wall Street Journal, p. A13.*

Jo, Hoje, and Na, Haejung (2012). Does CSR Reduce Firm Risk? Evidence from Controversial Industry Sectors. *Journal of Business Ethics*, Vol. 110(4), pp. 441-456.

Kaufman-Rosen, Leslie (October 17, 1994). Being Cruel to be Kind. *Newsweek*, p. 51.

Kickul, Jill, Terjesen, Siri, Bacq, Sophie, and Griffiths, Mark (September, 2012). Social Business Education: An Interview with Nobel Laureate Muhammad Yunus. The Academy of Management. Learning & Education, Vol. 11, No. 3, pp. 453-462.

Kramer, M. R. (2011). Shared Value vs. Don't be Evil. *Harvard Business Review*, Vol. 89, No. 7/8, pp. 18-19.

Kumar, P.S.S., Kuberudu, B., and Krishna, Srinivasa (January, 2011). Corporate Social Responsibility – Public Sensitivity. *Proficient*, pp. 7-13.

Lacovara, Christopher (2011). Strange Creatures: A Hybrid Approach to Fiduciary Duty in Benefit Corporations. *Columbia Business Law Review*, Vol. 2011, pp. 815-861.

Lawrence, Thomas, Phillips, Nelson, and Tracey, Paul (September, 2012). Educating Social Entrepreneurs and Social Innovators. The Academy of Management. *Learning & Education*, Vol. 11, No. 3, pp. 319-323.

Leisner, Richard M. (November, 1990). Florida's New Business Corporation Act. *The Florida Bar Journal*, pp. 9-15.

Liedtke, Michael (May 13, 2004). Gap vows to end plant abuses. *The Miami Herald*, pp. 1C, 4C.

Lindgreen, Adam, Maon, Francios, Reast, Jon, and Yani-De-Soriano (2012). Corporate Social Responsibility in Controversial Industry Sectors. *Journal of Business Ethics*, Vol. 110(4), pp. 393-95.

Lindorff, Margeret, Prior, Elizabeth Jonson, and McGuire, Linda (2012), Strategic Corporate Responsibility in Controversial Industry Sectors: The Social Value of Harm Minimization. *Journal of Business Ethics*, Vol. 110 (4), pp. 457-467.

Linn, Allison. (2007, April 18). *Corporations find business case for going green.* Retrieved from NBC News website: http://www.nbcnews.com/id/17969124/ns/business-going_green/t/corporations-find-business-case-going-green/#.UdtRrvlTBrs

Loten, Angus (January 19, 2012). With New Law, Profits Take Back Seat. *The Wall Street Journal*, pp. B1, B5.

Mackey, John, and Sisodia, Raj (2013). *Conscious Capitalism*. Boston: Harvard Business Review Press.

Maggins, Anastasia, and Tsaklanganos, Angelos A. (July/August, 2012). Predicting the Corporate Social Responsibility of Limited Liability Companies in Greece Using Market Variables. *The Journal of Applied Business Research*, Vol. 28, No. 4, pp. 661-671.

Marketing (August 8-12, 2012). Do-Gooder Retailing Goes Mainstream. *Business Week*, pp. 22-23.

Marx, Karl (1867). Capital vol. 1, trans. Ben Fowkes, New York: Vintage Books 1977

Mawdudi, Abul Aala (1996). The Making of Islamic Revivalism (New York: OUP).

McClatchy-Tribune News April 11, 2011). Socially responsible investing: Websites highlight how to do it. *Sun-Sentinel*, Money, p. 1.

McConnell, Beth (November 20, 2006). HR implements corporate social responsibility globally. *Society for Human Resource Management HR News*.

McKay, Betsy (March 15, 2007). Why Coke Aims to Slake Global Thirst for Safe Water. *The Wall Street Journal*, pp. B1, B2.

Merrick, Amy (May 12, 2004). Gap Offers Unusual Look at Factory Conditions. *The Wall Street Journal*, pp. A1, A12.

Minnesota Pollution Control Agency. (n.d.). *Become a paper-less office.* Retrieved from http://156.98.19.245/paper/Minnesota Pollution Control Agency. (n.d.). *Reducing waste in the workplace.* Retrieved from http://156.98.19.245/workplace/

Minnesota Statutes Section 302A.251(5) (2011).

Millward, L.J. and L.J. Hopkins 'Psychological contracts, organisational and job commitment', *Journal of Applied Social Psychology* (1998)28: 16–31.

Mickels, Alissa (Winter, 2009). Beyond Corporate Social Responsibility. *Hastings International and Comparative Law Journal*, Vol. 32, pp. 271-300.

Miller, Toyah L., Grimes, Matthew G., McMullen, Jeffrey S., and Vogus, Timothy J. (2012). Venturing for Others with Heart and Head: How Compassion Encourages Social Entrepreneurship. *Academy of Management Review*, Vol. 37, No. 4, pp. 616-640.

Millon, David (Fall, 2011). Two Models of Corporate Social Responsibility. *Wake Forest Law Review*, Vol. 46, pp. 523-35.

Mizruchi, Mark S., and Hirschman, Daniel (Summer, 2010). The Modern Corporation as Social Construction. *Seattle University Law Review*, Vol. 33, pp. 1065-1105.

Mujtaba, B. G. (2014). *Managerial Skills and Practices for Global Leadership.* ILEAD Academy: Florida.

Mujtaba, B. G. (2014). *Capitalism and its Challenges Across Borders (edited).* Florida: ILEAD Academy.

Mujtaba, B. G. (2007). *Mentoring Diverse Professionals (2nd edition).* Llumina Press. Davie, Florida, United States.

Mujtaba, B. G. and Cavico, F. J. (2013). A Review of Employee Health and Wellness Programs in the United States. *Public Policy and Administration Research*, 3(4), 01-15.

Mujtaba, B. G., and Cavico, F. J. (2013). Corporate Social Responsibility and Sustainability Model for Global Firms. *Journal of Leadership, Accountability and Ethics*, Vol. 10(1), pp. 58-76.

Mujtaba, B. G. and McCartney, T. (2010). *Managing Workplace Stress and Conflict amid Change, 2nd edition.* ILEAD Academy: Florida.

Mujtaba, B.G., Cavico, F.J.. and Acheraporn, P. (2012). Corporate Social Responsibility and Globalization. *Proceedings of the 17th International Conference of Asia Pacific Decision Sciences Institute (APDSI)*, Chaing Mai, Thailand. July 22-26, 2012.

Mujtaba, B. & Mujtaba, L. (March 2004). Diversity Awareness and Management in Adult Education. *Journal of College Teaching and Learning,* 1(3), 65-75.

Mujtaba, B. G. and Preziosi, R. C. (2006). *Adult Education in Academia: Recruiting and Retaining Extraordinary Facilitators of learning.* 2nd Edition. Information Age Publishing: Greenwich.

Munch, Steven (Winter, 2012). Improving the Benefit Corporation: How Traditional Governance Mechanisms Can Enhance the Innovative New Business Form. *Northwestern Journal of Law and Social Policy*, Vol.7, pp. 170-225.

Naik, Gautam (September 6, 2002). Glaxo to Cut Prices in Poor Countries. *The Wall Street Journal*, p. B1.

O'Connell, Vanessa (January 3, 2002). Landmark TV Liquor Ad Created by D.C. Insiders. *The Wall Street Journal*, pp. B1, B3.

O'Leary-Kelly, A.M. and J.A. Schenk (1999) '*An examination of the development and consequences of psychological contracts'*. Paper presented at the annual Meeting of the Academy of Management, Chicago.

Office Depot. (n.d.). *Top 20 Ways to Go Green at Work (and Save the University Money!)*. Retrieved from University of Washington website: http://www.washington.edu/admin/stores/eprocurement/office/green.pdf

Page, Antony, and Katz, Robert A. (Summer, 2011). Is Social Enterprise the New Corporate Social Responsibility. *Seattle University Law Review*, Vol. 34, pp. 1351-1384.

Paul, Sudhakar T. (January, 2012). Green Business or Sustainable Business: A Triple Bottom-line Approach. *Proficient*, pp. 78-87.

Pfeffer, J. (1995). Competitive advantage through people: Unleashing the power of the workforce. Boston, Harvard Business School Press.

Podsada, Janice (October 13, 2011). Handicrafts headed to Wal-Mart's website. *Sun-Sentinel*, p. 4D.

Porter, M.E. and Kramer, M.R. (2011). Creating Shared Value – How to Reinvent Capitalism and Unleash a Wave of Innovation and Growth. *Harvard Business Review*, Vol. 89, No. 1/2, pp. 63-77.

Porter, M.E. and Kramer, M.R. (2006). Strategy and Society: The Link between Competitive Advantage and Corporate Social Responsibility. *Harvard Business Review*, Vol. 84, pp. 78-92.

Pressman, Aaron (October 24, 2005). Activist Funds Make Waves. *Business Week*, p. 124.

Rashid, A.T. and Rahman, M. (2009). Making Profit to Solve Developmental Problems: The Case of Telenor AS and the Village Phone Program in Bangladesh. *Journal of Marketing Management*, Vol. 25, No. 9, pp. 1049-60.

Reich, Robert (September 10, 2007). It's Not Business' Business. *Business Week*, p. 86.

Reiser, Dana Brakman (Fall, 2011). Benefit Corporations – A Sustainable Form of Organization? *Wake Forest Law Review*, Vol. 46, pp. 591-620.

Resor, Felicia R. (2012). Benefit Corporation Legislation. *Wyoming Law Review*, Vol. 12, pp. 91-119.

Richards, Bill (May 13, 1998). Nike to Increase Minimum Age in Asia for New Hirings, Improve Air Quality. *The Wall Street Journal*, p. B10.

Rimanoczy, I. B. (2010). Business leaders committing to and fostering sustainability initiatives. *Doctoral dissertation*. Teachers College, Columbia University.

Rimanoczy, I. (2013). *Big Bang Being: Developing the Sustainability Mindset.* Sheffield, UK: Greenleaf Publishing.

Robinson, S.L. 'Trust and breach of the psychological contract', *Administrative Science Quarterly* (1996) 41:

Roche (2007). Sustainable Humanitarian Aid. Retrieved January 28, 2007 from: http://www.roche.com/home.sustainability/sus_csoc-resp/sus.

Rodgers, T.J. (April 30, 1997). Corporations' social responsibility: Increase profits. *The Miami Herald*, p. 11A.

Rodinson, Maxime (1973). Islam and Capitalism. New York: Pantheon Books

Rogers, Carl R. (1961). On Becoming a Person. Boston: Houghton Mifflin

Ronald McDonald House Charities of South Florida (February 9, 2012). Celebrating Thirty Years. *Sun-Sentinel*, Special Advertising Section.

Sadler, Philip (2010). *Consumption, Demand, and the Poverty Penalty*. Surrey, England: Gower Applied Research.

Sauser, Jr., William I. (2008). Regulating Ethics and Business: Review and Recommendations. SAM: Management in Practice, Vol. 12, No. 4, pp.1-7.

Schneitz, Karen E., and Epstein, Marc J. (Winter 2005). Exploring the Financial Value of a Reputation for Corporate Social Responsibility During a Crisis. *Corporate Reputation Review*, Vol.7, No. 4, pp. 327-45.

Schoops., Mark (January 14, 2004). HIV Test Makers Agree to Discounts for Poorer Nations. *The Wall Street Journal*, pp. B1, B2.

Schuler, Douglas A., and Cording, Margaret (2006). A Corporate Social Performance-Corporate Financial Performance Behavior Model for Consumers. *Academy of Management Review*, Vol. 31, No. 3, pp. 540-58.

Schwab, Klaus (January 15, 2010). Bank Bonuses and Communitarian Spirit. *The Wall Street Journal*, p. A19.

Shellenburger, Sue (October 13, 2005). Employers Begin to Provide Assistance for Parents of Children with Disabilities. *The Wall Street Journal*, p. D1.

Sherman, Richard W. (July/August, 2012). The Triple Bottom Line: The Reporting of "Doing Well" & "Doing Good." *The Journal of Applied Business Research*, Vol. 28, No. 4, pp. 672-682.

Shillington, Patty (June 16, 2008). Investors do well doing good. *The Miami Herald*, Business Monday, p. 13.

Smalley, Suzanne (December 3, 2007). Ben and Jerry's Bitter Crunch. Newsweek, p. 50.

Spector, Jonathan (2012). The Sustainability Imperative and Governance: Understanding a New Frontier in Corporate Board Oversight. *Notre Dame Journal of Law, Ethics, and Public Policy*, Vol. 26, pp. 39-44.

Swallow, Lisa, & Furniss, Jerry. (2011). *Green Business Reducing Carbon Footprint Cuts Costs and Provides Opportunities*. Retrieved from Bureau of Business and Economic Research The University of Montana website: http://www.bber.umt.edu/pubs/MBQ/greenbusinessarticle.pdf

Taqiuddin, al-Nabahani (2002). The economic System of Islam. New Delhi: Milli Publications.

Tasker, Fred (September 23, 2010). AIDS, HIV patients getting help from pharmaceutical companies. *The Miami Herald*, p. 5B.

Tasker, Fred (January 20, 2011). Funding gap threatens AIDS drug help. *The Miami Herald*, p. 5B.

Taylor, Celia R. (Summer, 2011). Berle and Social Businesses: A Consideration. *Seattle University Law Review*, Vol. 34, pp. 1501-20.

Tellus Institute. (2002). *Greening Your Products: Good for the environment, good for your bottom line.* Retrieved from US Environmental Protection Agency website: http://www.epa.gov/epp/pubs/jwod_product.pdf

The Environment Agency (n.d.). *Climate Change Agreements Scheme.* Retrieved from http://www.environment-agency.gov.uk/business/topics/pollution/136236.aspx

Tyagi, R.K. (November, 2011). A Conceptual Study of Corporate Social Responsibility and Its Persuasion on Employees. *Proficient*, pp. 2837.

Udgata, Jitarani and Das, Sarita (March 2012). Social Entrepreneurship: Challenges and Opportunities. *Tenecia Journal of Management Studies*, Vol. 6, No. 2, pp. 50-57.

Uwalomwa, Uwuigbe and Egbide, Ben-Caleb (March 2012). Corporate Social Responsibility Disclosures in Nigeria: A Study of Listed Financial and Non-Financial Firms. Journal of Management and Sustainability, Vol. 2, No. 1, pp. 160-69.

Wang, Heli and Qian, Cuili (2012). Corporate Philanthropy and Corporate Financial Performance: The Roles of Stakeholder Response and Political Access. *Academy of Management Journal*, Vol. 54, No. 6, pp. 1159-1181.

Windham, Christopher (March 29, 2004). J&J to Give Away New AIDS Drug. *The Wall Street Journal*, p. B6.

Workplace Visions (2007). Social Responsibility and HR Strategy. *Society for Human Resource Management*, No. 2, pp. 2-8.

World Bank Institute (2007). Internet Course: "CSR and Sustainable Competitiveness." Retrieved January 27, 2007 from: www.infoworldbank.org/etools/wbi_learning/index.

World Wide Fund for Nature. (n.d.). *How to reduce paper consumption in your office (and save money at the same time!).* Retrieved from http://awsassets.panda.org/downloads/final_paper_saving_tips_1.pdf

Author Biography

Frank J. Cavico is a Professor of Business Law and Ethics at the H. Wayne Huizenga School of Business and Entrepreneurship of Nova Southeastern University in Ft. Lauderdale, Florida. He has been involved in an array of teaching responsibilities, at the undergraduate, master's and doctoral levels, encompassing such subject matter areas as business law, government regulation of business, constitutional law, administrative law and ethics, labor law and labor relations, health care law, and business ethics. In 2000, he was awarded the Excellence in Teaching Award by the Huizenga School; and in 2007, he was awarded the Faculty Member of the Year Award by the Huizenga School of Business and Entrepreneurship; and in 2012 he was again honored by the Huizenga School as Faculty Member of the Year. Frank Cavico holds a J.D. from the St. Mary's University School of Law and an LL.M from the University of San Diego, School of Law; and is a member of the Florida and Texas Bar Associations. He is the author and co-author of several books and numerous law review and management journal articles.

Contributor Biographies

Muhammad Zeb Khan is Assistant Professor at FAST-National University, in Pakistan. His teaching experience is spread over twelve years with core competencies in the HRM and Project Management fields He attained a Masters of Commerce "with distinction"; and is now pursuing a Ph.D. in Management from the University of Punjab (Pakistan). His areas of research interest include Public Sector Reforms, with special focus on HRM. He has been regularly contributing articles on socio-economic issues to the daily "The News International."

Bahaudin G. Mujtaba is Professor of Management and Human Resources at the H. Wayne Huizenga School of Business and Entrepreneurship of Nova Southeastern University in Ft. Lauderdale, Florida. Bahaudin Mujtaba is the author and coauthor of twenty professional and academic books dealing with management, diversity, business ethics, and cross-cultural management, as well as over 200 academic journal articles. During the past thirty years he has had the pleasure of working with human resource professionals in the United States, Brazil, Bahamas, Afghanistan, Pakistan, St. Lucia, Grenada, Malaysia, Japan, Vietnam,

China, India, Thailand, and Jamaica. This diverse exposure has provided him many insights in ethics, culture, and management from the perspectives of different firms, people groups, and countries. Bahaudin can be reached at: mujtaba@nova.edu

Isabel Rimanoczy, Ed.D. is a Legacy Coach, working with people who want to make a difference. She is the author of Big Bang Being: Developing the Sustainability Mindset (2013), and teaches Sustainability Mindset at Fordham University, New York. She has made her life purpose to develop change accelerators, and does this by teaching, writing, running workshops for corporate leaders, coaching and public speaking. She is Director and co-founder of the charitable organization Minervas, Women Changing the World, that promotes self-managed groups of women wanting to make a difference. Her website is www.legacycoaching.net

Seeting "Grace" Zaelor, has an undergraduate degree in Business Administration from the Institute of International Studies at Ramkhamhaeng University, in Bangkok, Thailand. Zaelor obtained an Associate degree in Computer Science from Laguardia Community College in New York. She has been a Website Administrator for an artist since 2008. After completing her Associate degree in 2011, she worked as an Academic Peer Instruction Tutor for six months at Laguardia Community College before working as an Accounting Assistant at a restaurant in downtown Manhattan until August, 2012. Grace can be reached at: szc.grace@gmail.com

Index

Hawaii · 71
How to Do Good · 33, 144
Howard Schulz · 129
HR Magazine · 36, 41, 145
Huizenga School blog · 142
Human resource management · 99
Human Resource Management · 4, 45, 53, 99, 100, 142, 143, 147, 151
Human resources · 100
Humane Society · 33
Hurricane Katrina · 14
hypocrite · 104

I

IB327 course · 89
IBM · 59, 124
Idaho · 65
incongruence · 103
India · 32, 41, 45, 50, 51, 52, 59, 142, 153
Indian Oil Company · 51
Information technologies · 92
Institute of International Studies · 89, 153
Instrumental · 8, 17
intellectual acknowledgment · 134
intentions · 108
Intrinsic · 2, 8, 17
Investopedia · 57
ipso facto · 15
Islam · 99, 101, 103, 104, 108, 110, 111, 142, 150, 151

J

Jamaica · 153
Japan · 152
Jean-Pierre Garner · 42
Jerry Greenfield · 29
John Brown · 35

K

Katz · 25, 68, 72, 74, 75, 76, 81, 149
Khan · 99, 152
Klaus Schwab · 119
Kramer · 26, 27, 146, 149

L

L3C · 4, 81, 113
Laguardia Community College · 153
Lahore · 37
land pollution · 91, 93
last resort · 13, 15
Last Resort · 13
Laws · 9
Lead by example · 128
left brain · 134
Legacy Coach · 129, 153
legal requirements · 28, 48, 109
legal sanctions · 10
Legality · 139
limited liability company · 81
LLC · I, II, 81
Low-Profit Limited Liability Company · 4

M

Maggins · 28, 30, 32, 35, 147
Malaysia · 152
Manhattan · 153
Maryland · 71, 73
Masters of Business Administration · 39
MBA students · 133, 135
McClatchy-Tribune News · 56, 147
Mediterranean · 17
Mexico · 45, 59
Microsoft · 36, 94
Millennium Development Goals · 124, 143
Millon · 26, 27, 36, 46, 62, 63, 116, 148
Milton · 23, 50
Minervas · 153
Ministry of Corporate Affairs · 51
Minnesota Statutes Section · 63, 148
Mission Zero · 129
Model B-Corp Act · 71
Mohammad Yunus · 69
monopolist · 21
moral conclusions · 8
moral duty · 2, 13, 14, 15, 28
Moral philosophy · 10
Moral rules · 11
Moral standards · 11
Moral values · 9
Morality · 2, 7, 11, 19, 110
Morals · 11

Mujtaba, B. · II, 143, 148, 152
Mujtaba, Bahaudin · II
Muslim · 104, 105, 106, 108, 109, 110
Muslims · 100, 101, 103, 104, 105, 107, 108, 109

N

natural resources · 27, 89, 90, 93, 94, 96
NBC television · 34
Nestle Company · 47
New Jersey · 25, 71
New Orleans · 14
New York · 59, 71, 143, 145, 147, 150, 153
Newark · 25
Newsweek · 29, 146, 150
NGO · 52, 131
Nike · 34, 149
Nobel Laureate · 23
noise pollution · 93
nonprofit · 68, 74, 75
Normative stakeholders · 28
North Carolina · 71
Nova Southeastern University · 152

O

Obligation · 15
Oregon · 71

P

Pakistan · 37, 99, 152
Pennsylvania · 62, 64, 71
PepsiCo · 41, 43, 59
Persian · 20
Persuasive · 18
Peshawar · 99
philanthropy · 25, 30, 57
Philosophy · 10
plug-the-gap · 99
Political campaigning · 75
Pollutions · 93
Porter · 26, 27, 149
Preservation of water · 92
principles · 8, 10, 11, 19
Prius hybrid automobile · 26

Prophet · 104, 108, 110
Protagoras · 19
Protestant work ethic · 104
psychological contract · 100, 101, 102, 103, 146, 150
Public Interest Company · 76
public opinion · 10, 18

Q

Quran · 101, 103, 104, 105, 108, 109, 110, 111

R

Ramkhamhaeng University · 89, 153
Ray Anderson · 129
rebellious · 135
Reducing the electricity bill · 92
Rehman · 38, 142
Reich · 24, 149
reneging · 103
Republican · 23
Rhetoric · 18
Rimanoczy, I · 129, 150, 153
Rockefeller · 21
Roman · 20
Ronald McDonald · 31, 150
Royal Caribbean Cruise Company · 46

S

sadness · 135
Sal Paulo · 41
Schein · 102
SEC regulations · 84
Secretary of State · 73
self-fulfillment · 99, 101, 104, 107, 111
Self-fulfillment · 107
self-satisfaction · 18
Shahada · 109
shareholder-investors · 55
SHRM · 45
Social entrepreneurship · 68, 70
social or environmentally positive initiatives · 129
Social responsibility · 2, 10, 11, 15, 30, 114, 139, 140
Social Responsibility · 23